Reviews of 'Jesus is God, alwa will be!'

This is an excellent book. Although ... o
those with theological training, this book will be
especially helpful to the man on the street. The
believer will benefit greatly from a study of this short
volume. Looking forward to Part 2 in this series.

Dr. James McConnell
Senior Pastor
Whitewell Metropolitan Tabernacle
Belfast, N. Ireland

A "must read" for every child of God.
For learning, for reference and for growing in the
grace and knowledge of our Lord and Savior Jesus
Christ.
Martin Jordan, Wexford, Ireland.

Miles McKee has written a superb treatise on this
lofty theme. It is a
pleasure to read. You could preach a series of
sermons from this electronic
manuscript. His arguments are succinct and effective.
Christ is magnified in
His deity and humanity, without one eclipsing the
other. I highly recommend
this book.
Ben, Arizona, USA

I enjoyed reading McKee's book not simply because I agree with it but also because, with humor and good sense, he exposes the thoughts that keep us from enjoying the fullness of God. If I had prehensile feet I would give this book four thumbs up!

Bob Kilpatrick, California, USA. Singer/Songwriter, Public speaker and Author

In his book, Pastor Miles McKee has given a thorough, yet concise, explanation of the glorious truth of the Deity of Christ. I pray that this short book will be mightily used in evangelism to the glory of God.

Dr. John Killian
Pastor Maytown Baptist Church, Alabama
1st Vice President Alabama Baptist State Convention

Miles McKee is one of my very favorite preachers and missionaries. He has an exuberant passion for the gospel truth that exalts the crucified Savior, Jesus Christ, and glorifies God almighty.
Brother Miles is Biblical in his assertions, historical in his citations, accessible in his presentation, and God-glorifying in His proclamation. We would have expected no less from a man whose sole mission (and soul mission) is to "make Jesus famous" wherever he goes (and encourage the brethren to do likewise).

I most highly recommend this book to anyone who wants to draw nearer the heart of the heavenly Father through the truth of the eternal Son.

Jon Cardwell, Alabama, USA. Author, Pastor and

Bible Teacher

"If I ever find myself needing a Daniel Webster, I'm calling Miles McKee!"
Miles has now put forth a book which has as it's mission, a compelling argument for Jesus' being the holy ground zero of the Christian faith. Jesus is indeed God. Based on the Gospel Truth!"
Gordon Kennedy
Multi Grammy Award winning songwriter/musician/producer

This book is dedicated to my Mother and Father, Charles and Edna McKee who lived quietly in Maghera, Co. Derry, Northern Ireland, at peace with both God and man.

The Deity of Christ: Keep Calm because Jesus is God!

(Part 1)

Introduction.

1) The Dual Nature of Christ.

2) The Humanity of Christ.

3) His Deity.

4) So What's in a Name?

5) Some Common Theories and Objections Answered.

Introduction

I've wanted to write a series of books on the subject of the Deity of Christ for some time now. What sparked it was that I was ministering, a few years back, with my dear friend Dr. Joel Freeman of the Freeman Institute. It was 'meetings' at night and 'greetings' during the day.

Being out and about on one particular afternoon, we stopped for lunch at a small restaurant and, being as the weather was pleasant, sat down at an outside table. During lunch, I observed two young men moving from table to table, talking to the diners. Eventually they stopped with us. "Hi guys," they beamed, "we are Christians and in 15 minutes time we will be having a Bible study over by the fountain. We'd sure like to have you join us" "Christians?" I inquired of them with face covered by a puzzled look. "Oh yes," they responded with firmness, "we are Christians." I don't know what exactly happened at that point, but I smelt a rat. They troubled something deep within me. Just then inspiration hit. I knew I needed to draw them out and make them identify themselves so I said with a sneering tone, *"Christians! Don't tell me that you believe all that nonsense about Jesus being God?"* They looked knowingly at one another then at me and said, *"Well no, actually we don't believe that Jesus is God. We believe he is only the Son of God."*

"Gotcha!" I smiled and launched into a proclamation of the gospel. I told them in no uncertain terms of how the
God who had made all flesh and blood had Himself become flesh and blood in order to redeem ruined sinners at the Cross. I gave them an earful, and they were "sore discomforted" and by fleetness of foot secured their hasty flight to the relative safety of the far side of the courtyard.

There are two doctrines that the Devil hates with a passion, both of which are essential to the gospel. The first is Justification by grace through faith. The second is the Deity of the Lord Jesus Christ. Remember this, the Prince of Darkness hates Christ and is fully determined to blur and plunder His work and identity. His purpose is to blind unbelievers to prevent them from seeing the glory of the sufficiency of the gospel and the deity of the Redeemer. In 2 Corinthians 4:4 we read,

" --- the god of this world (Satan) hath blinded the minds of them which believe not, lest the light of the glorious gospel of Christ, who is the image of God, should shine unto them."

One of the marks of the unsaved is that they cannot see the glory of God in the person of Christ. Believers, on the other hand, have been given the light of the knowledge of the glory of God in the face of Jesus Christ (2 Corinthians 4:4). God's glory, God Himself, is known, only in Christ Jesus who is, "the brightness of

His (God's) glory, and the express image of His person (Hebrews 1:3). The glory of the gospel, therefore, is that the One who undertook our redemption is none other that the Eternal and Mighty God.

If we reject the deity of Christ we have no gospel for Jesus not only taught good news about God, He is the good news of God. He is the centre of the gospel, the full and final revelation from heaven. He is God's good news about Himself; to reject Him is to reject God: to deny His deity is to deny the deity of God Himself; to reject God's unveiling of Himself in Christ Jesus is to deny and pervert the gospel!

In the following pages, we will see the Scriptures are clear about Christ's identity. Gospel believers see that Christ is the revelation, image and manifestation of God. The mystery of God has been revealed: our blindness to this epic truth has been removed by grace. When Christ returns, we will see, in Him, the full display of the glory of God (I Timothy 6:14-16).

Many Christians do not know how to defend the Deity of Christ. This book is written for them. It is not written for the theologian, but rather for, as the antiquated expression has it, the 'man in the pew'. It is written in the hopes that it will equip many Christians to defend and honour Christ Jesus by proclaiming His Deity.

In my many talks through the years with Jehovah Witnesses (from hereon referred to as JWs) and others who deny the deity of Christ, they assure me that they get most of their recruits from born again

Christians. The 'born-agains', they tell me, are easy pickings for, although they are interested in the things of God, they don't know and study the Bible. What a scathing indictment, and yet, not without merit!

If we will take time to study these passages of Scripture or memorize them, we will never again have to fear confrontation with a J. W. or with members of any one of the many groups that, while they praise Christ, actually plunder Him by denying His Deity.

Chapter 1:

The Dual Nature Of Christ

At the outset, I need to state that this is not a book about the Trinity. I leave that subject to those with mightier pens than I. This is, however, a book about the identity of Jesus Christ, and if ever we are to understand the Lord Jesus we must grasp that He is one person with two natures: He is fully human yet fully divine. He is not a little bit human and a little bit God. He is fully human yet fully God. But how is that possible---- fully man yet fully God? Well, on that subject, I take sides with the old Irish preacher who said he'd not been sent to explain the gospel, but rather to proclaim it. That God became a man is something the Bible declares rather than explains. This hypostatic union, as the theologians call it, is a thrilling truth and the precise heart of the gospel. Some religions, such as Islam, reject this idea saying that God has no Son. But at the core of the Good News we discover it was the one true and living God who appeared in Bethlehem as a baby. The angels were astonished and broke out in unrestrained praise and adoration saying, *"Glory to God in the highest."* They were staggered and amazed for they could see that at the same time as this infant lay in Bethlehem's manger, He was upholding the universe with the word of His power.

The truth is, God does not owe any of us an explanation about anything. God can declare whatever He will without any obligation to explain Himself. That the Scriptures, as we will demonstrate, declare Christ Jesus to be both God and man is perfectly obvious. We can dismiss this idea and fly in the face of the evidence, but that will not alter the truth that the invisible God has objectified Himself and become visible in the person of the Lord Jesus Christ. So let's say it again, to understand Christ Jesus properly it is essential to grasp that He is both God and man.

He is one person with two natures. He is fully human and at the same time fully divine. In His power and wisdom, God became man without ceasing to be God. He did not become partly man and partly God, but was, in the person of Christ Jesus, fully God and fully man.

It is as we learn to distinguish between when Christ is talking and acting as a man or talking and acting as God that we mature in our understanding of who he is.

A. A. Hodge writes, "------ undoubtedly we freely admit—that in the constitution of the Person of the God-man lies the--- absolutely insoluble mystery of godliness.

How is it possible that the same Person can be at the same time infinite and finite, ignorant and omniscient, omnipotent and helpless? How can two complete spirits coalesce in one Person? How can two consciousnesses, two understandings, two memories, two imaginations, two wills, constitute one Person? All this is involved in the scriptural and Church doctrine of the Person of Christ. Yet no one can explain it. The numerous attempts made to explain or to expel this mystery have only filled the Church with heresies and obscured the faith of Christians."
A.A Hodge: The Person of Christ.

Chapter 2:

His Humanity.

Here are some of the scriptural proofs concerning his true humanity. (I quote them to show the scriptures declare Christ to be an actual human being and not merely some phantom appearing in the form of man.) Again let me stress, if we reject that God became human we are rejecting the gospel; indeed, we have no gospel. It was a man who died for us, a sinless man who was also God. Let's see what Dr. Luke has to say on the subject of the true and genuine humanity of the Lord Jesus.

Luke 2:40: "And the child grew, and waxed strong in spirit, filled with wisdom: and the grace of God was upon him."

Luke 2:52: *"And the child increased in wisdom and stature."*

In both these scriptures, Christ Jesus is plainly called a child, indeed a child who was both growing and increasing. This is a testimony that He was human for, as you know, God does not grow or increase in wisdom---humans do! The cults point to these scriptures in an attempt to prove Christ was not God saying, *"See, here it makes it clear, Jesus can't be God because he is said to grow and increase".*

But these verses have nothing to do with his Deity they are, rather, verses to establish His indisputable humanity.

Furthermore, it is essential for us to realize that Jesus was a real and genuine human being. He went through all stages of development that children go through. He had to be fed and toilet trained. Someone had to teach Him how to read. And just like any normal child He would have eventually played with the other children in his street. He would have run errands for His parents and have had household chores to complete. At some stage of His life, He would have become aware of the opposite sex, though, we are not given any details of this. But this we know, He was a genuine human who was tempted in all points as we are, yet without sin (Hebrews 4:15).

If this offends us, it's because we do not believe that Jesus was genuinely human. I remember one young preacher being disgusted with an older preacher who had said that, just like everyone else, Jesus had to use the bathroom. Perhaps we are like that young minister and still have a sanitized picture of Jesus. Our Jesus, perhaps only looked human, but, in reality, He floated through His life immune to the feelings and bombardments which impact human beings every day. If this is what we think, we have not yet grasped that He was an actual human being. However,

just as it is heresy to deny His Deity so it is equally heresy to deny His true humanity. In fact, the humanity of Christ is one of the great pillars of our gospel faith.

J.C. Ryle says,

"One thing, however, is perfectly clear, and we shall do well to lay firm hold upon it. Our Lord partook of everything that belongs to man's nature, sin only excepted. As man He was born an infant. As man He grew from infancy to boyhood. As man He yearly increased in bodily strength and mental power, during His passage from boyhood to full age. Of all the sinless conditions of man's body, its first feebleness, its after growth, its regular progress to maturity, He was in the fullest sense a partaker. We must rest satisfied with knowing this. To pry beyond is useless. To know this clearly is of much importance. An absence of settled knowledge of it has led to many wild heresies."   J.C. Ryle: Commentary on Luke 2:40.

He was a genuine human! Have you ever noticed in Matthew 4:2 how we read of Christ being hungry? This was a genuine hunger that gripped his body. He was famished!

Does this mean He was not God? Not at all, it clearly demonstrates, once more, that He was human. Remember, He is fully man yet fully God.

As Isaac Watts wrote;

"Hosanna to the royal Son

Of David's ancient line!

His natures two, his person one,

Mysterious and divine."

In John 4: 6 we read of Christ being fatigued and exhausted after His long journey to Samaria. He experienced the same kind of weariness we would experience after such a long period of physical exercise. Again, this goes to show that He was human. The critics say, *"But how could He have been weary if He was God? Doesn't the Bible say that, the God of Israel neither faints nor gets weary?"* Of course it does! But Jesus, as God, did not get tired; it was Jesus, the man, who suffered the exhaustions of the human condition. The staggering truth is that although Jesus was God, He was also genuinely human and thus subject to human limitation. We need to write this truth large in our thinking; Christ Jesus is one person with two natures! Furthermore, in Matthew 8:24 we discover Christ sleeping. *"Wait a minute,"* say His enemies, *"this really proves that He was not God for,"* they say, *"the God of Israel neither slumbers nor sleeps."* Again, however, these would be troublers of the faith, fail to grasp that this scripture, and others like it, are there to establish His true humanity, not His Deity.

The same man who was hungry was the God who fed the five thousand. The same one who on the cross was parched with thirst, as God stands up and cries, "If any one thirst let him come unto Me and drink." The same man who was tired and slept, as God issues the invitation to the weary and heavy laden to come unto Him and rest! So if He is not God we are left with a man who gets hungry yet claims to be the bread of life: a man who gets thirsty yet tells us to come to him and drink and a man who gets weary yet tells us to come to him and rest. If these are not the words of God, this man Jesus is nuts! The only way to make sense of Jesus is to receive that He is both God and man! It was necessary that Christ should be a man for we needed someone to represent us. We needed a human being to live in our place. Why? Because all of us have sinned and have fallen short of God's holy standard----- that's why! When God came to earth, He came as one of us. He divested Himself of His glory, veiled his Deity and became our substitute in His birth, life, death and resurrection. It was a real man who lived for us; it was a real man who died in our place, and it is one of us, a real man, who now intercedes for us in Heaven.

We needed a life of perfect righteousness to present to God, and our flawed efforts did not make the grade. That's one of the principal reasons why Christ came.

He came as our substitute, the substitute man. If He were not a man, truly a man, then there is no gospel, no redemption and no salvation. It was man who had sinned and man who was guilty; therefore, it had to be one of us, a human representative who would take the punishment on our behalf. But more than that, we needed a representative, a human being to stand in our place and produce a perfect, flawless righteousness that could be reckoned as ours. An angel could not represent us or become our substitute in life and death. The representative had to be one of us, otherwise there is no good news. For there to be any gospel at all, Christ Jesus had to be one of our race, a human, descended from Adam. Adam, the first human being, as the head and representative of humanity, brought condemnation upon us all. Christ Jesus, in order to become the Last Adam, had to be totally human; He had to be one of us. We had to be rescued by one of our own! But where would God find such a human? Where would He find someone untainted with Adam's sin? His eyes ran throughout the whole world, and his verdict was, *"There is none righteous no not one, there's none that doeth good, there's none that understand, there's none that seeks God"* (Romans 3:10-11), *"their whole head is sick"* (Isaiah 1:5) and *"their heart is divided"* (Hosea 10:2). Man had been so totally ruined by sin and had fallen so far short of God's glory that no qualified redeemer could be found.

A qualified redeemer, by law, had to be a near kinsman therefore, since no perfect man could be found, God came here Himself and assumed a true and genuine human nature, became one of the human family, and yet remained God.

Some suggest that God merely possessed a man called Jesus and worked through him. This man, they say, was not God but a man filled perfectly with God. This, however, is an exceedingly silly notion!

There was no point in God taking a man and filling him with Himself for that man would still be a sinful descendant of Adam, ruined with human depravity. A depraved man could, therefore, never be a suitable and sinless substitute for us. Every human, without exception, was disqualified as a fitting substitute because every one of us had sinned. But, on the other hand, if the Redeemer had not been human there could have been no redemption. Likewise, if the redeemer had not been God, then no redemption could be accomplished for no mere man could absorb the wrath of God and live again. Indeed, if He had not been God, this redeemer would have been in need of a Saviour himself and, therefore, could have saved no one. God alone can save (Isaiah 43:11).

The great reformer, Theodore Beza, in his work, "Jesus Christ the Son of God", further explains God's genius in giving us the dual nature of Christ,

"---the wrath of God being infinite, there was no human or angelic strength known which could bear such a weight without being crushed (John 14:10, 12, 31; 16:32; 2 Corinthians. 5:19). He who was to live again, after having conquered the devil, sin, the world and death united to the wrath of God, had to be therefore not only perfect man, but also true God."

The genius of the dual nature of Christ is this, if He had been a mere man, He could not have conquered death. On the other hand, if He had been God only, He could not have died. The Lord Jesus, therefore, had to, of a necessity, be both God and man. As the God/Man, He lived, died and rose again on our behalf. As the sinless man, he took man's curse and condemnation and became liable for our sins. As God, He supplied His perfect humanity with the infinite power needed to absorb the fury of righteous wrath again our sin. What a glory there is in this gospel!

That Christ is both God and man is sheer and total genius. Martin Luther writes, "I often delight myself with the thought of a fishing hook that fishermen cast into the water, putting on the hook a little worm;

then comes the fish and snatches at the worm and gets the hook in his jaws and the fisherman pulls him out of the water.

 Even so has our Lord God dealt with the devil; God has cast into the world his only Son, as the fishing line, and upon the hook has put Christ's humanity, as the worm; then comes the devil and snaps at the (man) Christ, and devours him, and therewith he bites the iron hook, that is, the Godhead of Christ, which chokes him, and all his power thereby is thrown to the ground. This is called divine wisdom."
Martin Luther: The Smalcald Articles.

Substitute and Saviour

For Christ to become our saviour, all that he did would have to be done as our substitute -- in other words, done as if He were us. Christ's righteousness would not save us unless it was rendered to God as being ours. Christ, therefore, could not have become a genuine and effective substitute unless all that he accomplished on our behalf was carried out as a real human being. Justice demands righteousness from man; therefore, Christ's obedience had to be a genuine human obedience.

On the other hand, if Christ had been merely a human and only a human, His obedience would not have been that of a substitute, because He would have owed perfect obedience to God on His own behalf. However, Christ is the eternal God made human. As God, He was, therefore, man's Lawgiver and thus owed no obedience to a law which He had given to man. Obedience is the obligation of the creature, not that of the Creator. But Christ voluntarily assumed both our nature and our requirement for obedience so that in our place He accomplished that which was impossible for us --the fulfilling of the law. Christ Jesus, therefore, is both fully God and fully man. It could have been no other way. By not grasping the essence of redemption, the opponents of the gospel refuse to see this essential gospel truth.

They foolishly point to matters that belong to His ministry as the representative man and try to prove from these that He was not the Eternal One. A good example of this is when they point to His prayer life as a supposed proof that He was not God. *"Surely, God does not need to pray"* they say. Indeed not! God has no need of prayer, but man does. So, when we see Jesus praying, we see the representative man praying.

Furthermore, because we needed a perfect righteousness we needed, of a necessity, a perfect prayer life to present to God, and Jesus gave us one… His own. As our substitute, He prayed, not only for us, but also prayed as us.

In a similar way, all of us needed a perfect obedience to present to God, but, let's face it, not one of us has come close to being perfectly obedient to God. Christ, on the other hand, lived as our substitute and representative. His total obedience is now ours. His was the only perfect life. He was fully submitted to the Father, His will was totally subjected to the Father. This is the lifestyle that, as Christians, we all strive to have. We desire to have God first and foremost, but alas it doesn'tt always work out that way. Christ, by contrast, emptied Himself of the divine prerogatives, became a servant, submitted His will to that of the Father and became obedient unto death even the death of the cross (see Philippians. 2:5-11).

The opponents of Christ's divinity, not understanding the glory of the gospel, point to every instance where Christ Jesus, as our substitute, subjected Himself to the Father and say to us, *"See here, this man is not equal to God because He is in subjection to God."* They rise up like noisy, thankless children protesting that Christ, therefore, cannot possibly be God. Not understanding the gospel, they try to argue that since Christ is subordinate He must, therefore, be a created being who had a beginning! With great delight and salivating relish, they point to scriptures such as;

Luke 22:42, *"not my will but thine be done;"*

John 5:30, *"I seek not mine own will but the will of Him who sent me;"*

John 5:19, *"The Son can do nothing of Himself;"*

John 6:38, *"I came down from Heaven, not to do mine own will but the will of Him who sent me."*

However, the barren deficiencies of their understanding are exposed when they hurl insults and challenges at the Lord of Glory.

The enemies of Christ's deity have not yet grasped that we need a perfect righteousness to present in Heaven.

They do not seem to know that it is in the God/Man that this righteousness is found.

If they are not looking to Christ alone for perfect righteousness, they must then look for this righteousness, not in a substitutionary representative, but within themselves. They have not yet grasped that it is beyond our ability to deliver to God a level of perfection that will satisfy His holiness. In fact, denial of the dual nature of Christ always leads to the teaching of a works salvation. They cannot rest upon the accomplishments of Christ alone for, in their opinion, He is but a created being and not the everlasting God made flesh.

In summary, there would have been no salvation, no redemption and no upholding of God's justice had there been no God/Man. But, in the Lord Jesus Christ, the justice, holiness, love, goodness and saving power of God become visible in a genuine and true man. From this revelation of Christ we see, above all else, that God is personal. He is not just some marvellous power or mighty force; He is the God who has displayed Himself by becoming a man. And as a man, He was hungry (Matthew 4:2); thirsty (John 19:28); exhausted (John 4:6). As a man, He slept (Mark 4:38); was inundated with sorrow, (John 11:35); and tortured in His body (John 19:1—3); all these were evidences that Jesus was truly human. And yet this same human being could command trees to wither, storms to cease, loaves and fish to multiply, water to become wine, blind men to see, lame men to walk, the demons to flee, and the dead to come out of the grave.. And the reason he could do this was that He was fully God. In every respect, Christ Jesus lived a life that fully glorified God. It was a life that we had failed to live. Had the eternal Word not become human, He could not have lived a substitutionary and representative life that could be credited to our account. Now that we are in Christ, however, all that He has done for us is reckoned as having been done by us.

We now, in Christ, have a life of perfect prayer, perfect worship, perfect obedience, perfect submission and perfect love. If Christ was merely a spirit who looked like a man or was an angel impersonating man, then we are all lost.

We cannot be saved by a spook or represented by a phantom. It was a man, Adam, who had sinned and had caused the human race to be lost; it, therefore, had to be a man who would come to the rescue. Christ the last Adam, lived, died and rose again and by His accomplishments secured Salvation for His people.

"A man there is a real man,

With wounds still gaping wide,

From whom rich streams of blood once ran'

In hands and feet and side.

('Tis no wild fancy of our brain,

No metaphor we speak;

The same dear man in heaven now reigns

That suffered for our sake.)

This wondrous man of whom we tell,

Is true Almighty God;

He bought our souls from death and hell;

The price, His own heart's blood."

Joseph Hart.

Chapter 3

His Deity.

'Nothing is more fully and clearly revealed in the Gospel than that unto us Jesus is "the image of the invisible God;" that He is the character of the person of the Father, so as in seeing Him we see the Father also; that we have "the light of the knowledge of the glory of God in His face alone,"...This is the principal fundamental mystery and truth of the gospel; and if not received, believed, owned, all other truths are useless to our souls.'   John Owen (Vol. 1, Works, page 305).

"The very basis of Christianity is that Jesus was God manifest in the flesh (I Timothy 3:16). If that assertion can be overthrown, then the whole superstructure of Christianity crashes to the ground, and we are bound to assume that Jesus was either a shameless impostor or that He suffered from a delusion."   The Incomparable Christ: J. Oswald Sanders (p.53)

Although, Jesus was and is fully man, He is also *fully God*. If Jesus had merely been a man, a sinless man, but only a man, he could have only lived and died as a substitute for one sinful person, no more and no less. Legally, a human substitute cannot die in place of a multitude for by definition substitution places one person in place of another. An eye could be taken for an eye or a life for a life. However, there was a limit restricting these things. On the other hand, Jesus was not only the perfect man, He was the Mighty God. This means that He, as the source of life, can apply His atonement to as many as He desires. The substitutionary work of Christ in His doing and dying is thus endued with such sufficiency that it will affect every tribe, nation kindred and tongue (Revelation 5:9).

So, let's look and see where the Bible teaches that this man Christ Jesus is actually God. Let's start with John 1:1. There we are told that Jesus is the Eternal Word. This means He is God.

Jesus, the Eternal Word.

The Hymn writer, Isaac Watts, was staying faithful to Scripture when he penned these words

;"Ere the blue heav'ns were stretched abroad.

 From everlasting was the Word:

 With God he was; the Word was God,

And must divinely be adored."

But, how can we adore Christ Jesus if we do not realise that He is fully God? This is one of the compelling reasons why this glorious doctrine of the

 deity of Christ must be restored to prominence. For those starting out on a study of this great truth, John's Gospel is an excellent place to start. He commences by informing us,

"In the beginning was the Word, and the Word was with God, and the Word was God. The same was in the beginning with God. All things were made by him; and without him was not any thing made that was made." *(John1: 1-3).*

John 1:1 declares that Jesus was already there before the creation. This means that He is the Lord God. He was there in the beginning. When was the beginning? We don't know, but whenever it was it was not the beginning of Jesus. He was already there when the beginning happened. Jesus was not one of the created

things, He was the Word from eternity, not from time. But it says, *"The Word was with God"*---does this mean that He is less that God? Far from it, for God's word is His self-expression. Let's say, for example, that God had neither spoken nor expressed Himself, would that have meant that His Word was not with Him? Of course not, it would simply mean that His Word had not been yet manifest.

On the other hand, if He chose to express Himself would that mean that His self-expression had never existed before this? Of course not!

But, Christ Jesus is more than God's expression, He is God. When we express ourselves, we reveal our thoughts with words or actions.

My fellow countryman, Seamus Heaney, for example, expresses himself with words, but, marvellous as his poems are, no one would ever say that they are Seamus Heaney. The self-expression of writers reveals something about the writer, but they are not the writer. This is one of the many differences between ourselves and God. God's Word is His self-expression and is, in fact, Himself. Then our verse says, "And *the word was God*."

Arthur Pink observed, *"Not only was Christ the Revealer of God, but also He always was, and ever remains, none other than God Himself."* (Exposition of the Gospel of John: Chapter 2: Christ the Eternal Word).

Not only was our Saviour the One through whom, and

by whom, God has made Himself known

... but He Himself is God. Since the scriptures identify the Word as being the Lord Jesus, we should, as an experiment, try reading the first verses replacing the term 'Word' with 'The Lord Jesus Christ'.

It reads then as follows, *"In the beginning was the Lord Jesus Christ and the Lord Jesus Christ was with God and the Lord Jesus Christ was God."*

"And the Lord Jesus Christ was God." Need we say any more?

Remember, when dealing with the Lord Jesus we are dealing with the One who is both God and man. John Owen, the great puritan theologian writes, "The Word was made flesh and dwelt among us." But what Word was this? That which was in the beginning which was with God which was God by whom all things were made and without whom was not anything made that was made; who was light and life. This Word was made flesh not by any change of His own nature or essence, not by a transubstantiation of the divine nature into the human, not by ceasing to be what he was but by becoming what he was not, in taking our nature to his own, to be his own, whereby he dwelt among us." Owens Works: Vol. 1 p 46-47

John then goes on to say in John.1: 14,

*"And the Word was made flesh (*became human*) and dwelt among us."*

This is John's account of the Christmas Story. He informs us that the eternal Word became one of us.

Jesus, the eternal Word, is not a word about God, but is rather the Word who is God.

Notice how the Word, who was in the beginning, became human, and this same Word was God. *"The Word became flesh."* In the Greek language, the word for "flesh" is "sarx" which refers to human nature in its entirety. Christ did not simply take on the appearance of a man, He became thoroughly and utterly human in His mind will and emotions. Notice how John, writing by divine inspiration, offers no explanations for this. He is totally convinced that Jesus is the Eternal Word made flesh. He is fully persuaded that Jesus is both God and man. In this brief, telling statement

, "The Word was made flesh," John is not trying to introduce a new truth to the Christian community. If he were, he would have given a long exposition and explanation on the entire matter. He would, perhaps, have referenced the philosophical notion of the Word the Logos, and tried to explain how Plato said this or that and how that the Greeks were. Perhaps influenced by the Hebrew writings.

 But he says none of this! Apparently, there was no need to do so as the Christian community, in the first century, already believed the truth that the Logos, the Word, was God and that this Word had become flesh!

That the Word became flesh should fill our hearts with worship. It is no wonder that the hymn writer can say;

Thou art the everlasting Word,
The Father's only Son;
God manifest, God seen and heard,
The heaven's beloved One;
Worthy, O Lamb of God, art Thou,
That every knee to Thee should bow!
In Thee, most perfectly expressed,
The Father's self doth shine;
Fullness of Godhead, too: the Blest,

Eternally Divine;
Worthy, O Lamb of God, art Thou,
That every knee to Thee should bow!
Image of the Infinite Unseen

Whose being none can know;
Brightness of light no eye hath seen,
God's love revealed below;

Worthy, O Lamb of God, art Thou,

That every knee to Thee should bow!
Josiah Conder.

God has revealed Himself in the person of His Son. If the Word had not become flesh, we would not quite know what God is like! In the Old Testament, we were given specific names of God and sets of qualities such as Holiness, Justice, Wisdom, etc. If this information, though vital and helpful, were all that we had to construct a picture of God, our knowledge of Him would have been deficient. But the Word becoming flesh changes all of this. The Word has come to declare God unto us. Jesus has taken the guesswork out of God. As one young girl said, "Jesus is the best picture God ever had taken of Himself." Now, in Christ Jesus, we can know God and meet Him in a new and personal way! God has become one of us!

Jesus is the Creator ...That means He is God.

"All things were made by him; and without him was not any thing made that was made" John 1:3. Notice how John informs us that the 'Word' created everything.

Here, creation is ascribed to Him, for no one but *God* can create. This verse, therefore, declares the supreme deity of Jesus, the Christ! In many places, the Bible clearly says that God created everything. Here are but a few.

Genesis 1:1 "In the beginning God created the heaven and the earth."

Genesis 1:21 "And God created great whales, and every living creature that moves."

Genesis 1:27 "-- God created man in his own image, in the image of God created he him; male and female created he them." (see also Gen 2:4,Isa 45:18;40:28; Mal 2:10).

So, follow the logic. The Bible says that God created all things. It also says that Christ Jesus created all things. Therefore, if Jesus is not God, we have two creators. Conversely, if we have only one creator and Jesus Christ is not He, then the Bible is wrong and inaccurate.

Take your pick, either Jesus is God, or the Bible is not reliable. As we study the Scriptures; however, it becomes clear that Jesus and God are one and the same. If this were not so, Paul could not have written the following;

'For by him (Jesus) were all things created, that are in heaven, and that are in earth, visible and invisible, whether they be thrones, or dominions, or principalities, or powers: all things were created by him, and for him: And he is before all things, and by him all things consist. (Colossians 1:16-17).

What Paul is telling us in these verses is that Christ created and sustains all things. In the light of this scripture, how can anyone say that Jesus is not God? If Jesus is not God,

what exactly has God been doing with His time?

How does he occupy Himself? He is obviously in retirement or on the golf course for someone else is sustaining the universe and doing His job for Him!

Furthermore, note also how Paul, in this verse, says that Christ 'is' before all things---not 'came to be' before all things. Paul is telling us that Christ Jesus always 'is'------ And the One who *'is before all things'*, the Lord Jesus Christ, is the same one who created all things and is, therefore, God.

It should also be noted that the JWs changed this verse. According to them, at some point in eternity Jesus was created and then, as the agent of Jehovah, He created all other things. The Bible, however, knows nothing of this for observe how it simply says that Jesus created all things. If Jesus is created, He is, according to this verse, a "thing". But the Bible tells us that the Lord Jesus created all "things." So to be consistent with their theory, the JWs then would have to admit that Jesus created Himself. Created Himself? That would be an exceptionally challenging feat for anyone to attempt, never mind achieve!

But still they come back at us, insisting that, yes indeed, Jesus was God's agent in the creation. Try telling that one to Isaiah!   In Isaiah 44:24 we read,

"I am the LORD that maketh all things; that stretches forth the heavens alone; that spreads abroad the earth by myself;"

Notice, how God Almighty has no junior partner in His marvellous enterprise of creation! Yahweh clearly states that He created the heavens without the aid, help or agency of any other. God is the only creator. Man, with all his boasting, is unable to create anything. Man can make, but not create!

To create something we have to start with nothing and make something. That's the way God did it! Man, for all his genius, cannot do this. He must have something to start with before he makes his 'creation'. To make a table, for example, he needs materials. But, to be able to take nothing and make something is a skill which God has reserved exclusively for Himself. He is the only one who can take nothing and make something out of it. Only omnipotence can do this, and God cannot delegate His omnipotence to anyone. If He could do this, then the person to whom He delegated omnipotence would become God. This would leave us with two Gods ---an event that the living and true God will not allow. We again must conclude, therefore, that either the Bible is lying to us when it tells us that Christ Jesus created all things, or that it is telling us that Jesus and God are one and the same.

Isaac Watts captured this truth when he wrote,

"By his own power were all things made;

By him supported all things stand;

He is the whole creation's head,

And angels fly at his command."

The Lord Jesus Christ is The Eternal One...that means He is God!

"The eternity of Christ is the ground of the Christian religion." (Stephen Charnock: Works, Vol.1, p. 361).

Only God Himself is Eternal. If Christ can be seen to be eternal, then our case for His Deity is once more proven. On the other hand, if He had a beginning, He who was Christ cannot be God. If there ever was a time when He who was Christ was not, then he was and is not the Eternal God.

We have already seen that He is the eternal Word, so strictly speaking nothing more needs to be said on this point. However, just for a moment, let's look further at the eternality of the Word.

John 1:1-3 makes it abundantly clear that the Lord Jesus had no beginning, *"In the beginning was the word etc."* Draw the curtain of time back and there stands Jesus, the Eternal Word and Creator of all things! Now, let's ask the prophet Micah has he anything to add to this matter.

Micah 5:2, *"But thou, Bethlehem Ephratah, though you be little among the thousands of Judah, yet out of you shall he come forth unto me that is to be ruler in Israel; whose goings forth have been from of old, from everlasting."*

Of course, the critics say that this is evidently not Jesus of whom the prophet is speaking. *'When Jesus came to earth'*, they reason, *'He did not rule in Israel. He was not the King of the Jews, that position was occupied by Herod.'*

Actually, the truth is that, in spite of Herod reigning in Israel at that time, Christ Jesus was the true King of the Jews. The wise men asked, "Where is he that is born King of the Jews." Christ was born a King, however, as we know, all too well, the people rejected His kingship saying, *"We will not have this man to rule over us."* They knew His claims were claims of sovereign rulership for they protested, *"We have no King but Caesar."* And while it is true that Israel, as a nation, rejected His rulership and put Him on the cross, even there at the cross, we see Christ's Kingship shining through. Remember how Pilate affixed the sign to the cross that read, *"Jesus of Nazareth King of the Jews."*

Perhaps he did this to annoy the Jewish leaders, perhaps he had more insight than we credit him for, but regardless of why he did it, he gave us a declaration of Christ's true identity. Notice how regal Christ was even in death! Notice how, at the cross, King Jesus took that which looked like shame and failure and turned it into triumph! He was every inch a King!

The cross instead of being a mournful failure was transformed into Christ's greatest victory! It was a victory for light over darkness, a victory of divine love and grace! Satan was routed, death destroyed, and justice carried the day! Through the blood of the cross, King Jesus made peace (Colossians 1:20) and reconciled all things to Himself (Colossians 1:20).

Indeed, as Christ hung upon the cross with the lifeblood dripping from his body, He transformed the cross into a throne from which He ruled and reigned. To one thief He gave mercy and granted eternal life; to the other, by His silence, He decreed banishment and exclusion. He decided who lived and who died: this is the right of a King. As Dr. Desmond Ford writes,

"It is from the cross that Christ sways the hearts of men and conquers them. Conquering is a king's business! It is when we see him hanging there writhing in tortured agony for our sins that he overcomes our resistance to His love. Israel according to the flesh may have rejected Him but through the centuries there has been a spiritual Israel composed of all who believe over whom He rules and reigns and exercises His gracious Kingdom government." (Dr. Desmond Ford: A Kaleidoscope of Diamonds).

The Everlasting Father

Jesus Christ is the everlasting Father, that means He is God. The majestic prophet Isaiah again establishes the eternality of Christ by saying in Isaiah 9:6-7, *'For unto us a child is born, unto us a son is given: and the government shall be upon his shoulder:*

and his name shall be called Wonderful, Counselor, The mighty God, The everlasting Father, The Prince of Peace."

This scripture is one of the clearest declarations of the dual nature of Christ (His humanity and deity). The child who was born was both the Mighty God and the Everlasting Father. John Owen, the famous Puritan says,

"He is called, in the first place, Wonderful and that deservedly: Proverbs 30:4. That the Mighty God should be a child born and the Everlasting Father a Son given unto us may well entitle him to the name Wonderful." John Owen: The Works of John Owen: Volume One: Chapter 3: p47 The Banner of Truth Trust.

He is both Wonderful and Everlasting! It doesn't get much plainer than that. One has to change the text (as indeed some have) to avoid the grand conclusion that Christ is indeed God. Every attribute of deity is found in Him—omnipotence, omniscience, omnipresence.

The disciples were so stunned by Him that they asked one another, 'What manner of man is this that even the waves obey him?' But, so great is the mystery of Christ that He is the child and the mighty God all at the same time! We may not understand how He can be both, but Isaiah plainly states the facts of the matter.

Furthermore, do you see how the text declares His eternity? He is the Everlasting Father! Some have rendered this as the Father of Eternity others say it should be translated Author of Eternity. Call it any way you like, it doesn't matter, His Godhead is proved. We may not understand how this truth can be so, but the Bible plainly states it and, therefore, we should believe.

Spurgeon throws some excellent light on the eternity of Christ in his sermon on this passage saying;

'He is here pictured as the source and Father of eternity. Jesus is not the child of eternity but the Father of it. Eternity did not bring him forth from its mighty bowels, but he brought forth eternity. Independent, self-sustained, uncreated, eternal existence is with Jesus our Lord and God'   CHS: His Name, The Everlasting Father: Sermon # 724. In Conclusion, He who was the Christ is eternal. The Scriptures are clear on this matter.

Therefore, once more we see that Christ Jesus is God manifest in the flesh.

The Mighty God

At the Council of Chalcedon in A.D. 451 the Church affirmed that Christ was one person with two natures. Christ, they said, was fully God and fully man. However, the teaching of Chalcedon was no 5th century invention. This was no, *"figment of pious imagination"* for the mighty prophet Isaiah had already given the same key to understanding the mysterious constitution of the person of Christ. Let's look again at what he says;

"Unto us a child is born."

So, before we go any further, let me ask you, is a child which is born a human? Of course it is! But Isaiah goes on to declare that this child is also, "The Mighty God." This child is given the full title of Deity being called '*el gibbor'*, the Mighty God. This is a name reserved for God alone for in Isaiah 10:20-21, we see that it is Yahweh Himself who is this 'el gibbor'.

"And it shall come to pass in that day, that the remnant of Israel, and such as are escaped of the house of Jacob, shall no more again stay upon him that smote them; but shall stay upon the LORD, the Holy One of Israel, in truth. The remnant shall return, even the remnant of Jacob, unto the mighty God (el gibbor)."

According to Deuteronomy 6:4, there is one LORD; thus the child born is Yahweh clothed in humanity. The Child of Isaiah 9:6 and the LORD are one and the same! This child of the manger is 'el gibbor,' the Mighty God. For God to be God He must have all might, all power and all sovereignty. So let me ask, how many mighty Gods are there? I hope you don't think there is more than one! I'm reminded of the wee man at a prayer meeting who, speaking from the depth of his ignorance proclaimed *"The Devil is almighty, but our God is even more almightier."* That comment earned the poor chap a well-deserved round of muffled merriment. Obviously, there is no such thing as the Almighty and the Almightier! The Bible and logic know of only one Almighty God, and the scriptures declare that this mighty God and the Lord Jesus (the child born) are one and the same! If we believe that Christ is human, but not the Mighty God, then we reject the clear record of the Bible. We are treating the Bible like a giant cafeteria where we can pick and chose the things we like! However, Isaiah in this one scripture (Isaiah 9:6) has given us the key to unlock the mystery of Christ's identity. This promised one is to be both God and man, both human and divine, or as we have already discovered, one person with two natures. This key opens up the door and reveals Christ's person. If you throw this key away,

you will remain shut out and remain in the dark when it comes to understanding the identity of Christ.

Nothing More Than a First Name?

Critics, especially the Muslims, say that the term, "Mighty God", is just a name and nothing more than a first name given by his parents to the coming Prophet (Jesus). They say, had Isaiah 9:6 said something like, *"and he will be God Almighty Himself"*, then this would be different for we would now be talking about, not merely a child's name given in honour of God, but rather about GOD Almighty Himself.

This, of course, is an uncommonly silly argument, as no self- respecting Hebrew parent would have named their child 'God'---never mind, 'The Mighty God'. For example, a Jewish child might have been called Eldad which means "the favour of God", or they might have called their child Eliakim which means "God raises", or they may even have named a boy Elijah which means "Yahweh is my God". But nowhere do we ever find a Jewish boy running around the place being named El Gibbor, "The Mighty God". Besides that, Isaiah, it must be remembered, was not naming the child. The Father was doing the naming as the prophet wrote by inspiration of the Spirit. Here's a heart warming word from the powerful pen of Spurgeon on this matter,

"..........come and put your trust in Jesus Christ, he is "the mighty God." Oh, Christians, believe him more than ever, cast your troubles constantly on him; he is "the mighty God;" go to Him in all your dilemmas, when the enemy comes in like a flood, this mighty God shall make a way for your deliverance;

take to him your griefs, this mighty God can alleviate them all; tell him your backslidings and sins, this mighty God shall blot them out." CHS: His Name---- The Mighty God: Sermon #258.

Jesus is the Mighty God! If you do not believe this, yet you are trusting Jesus to save you, you have placed your trust in someone who, in your estimation, is less than God. It is with sadness that I tell you that you are following a different Christ than the one revealed in God's Word. With respect, we must conclude that your Christ is a Christ of human imagination and invention. The awful thing about this is that your Christ cannot save you. With a Saviour less than divine you have a limited Saviour who cannot save to the uttermost for He is not the Mighty God! Listen again to Watts,

> "The virgin's promised Son is born,
>
> Behold the expected child appear:
>
> What shall his names or titles be?

"The Wonderful, the Counsellor."

[This infant is the mighty God,

Come to be suckled and adored;

The eternal Father, Prince of Peace,

The Son of David, and his Lord.]"

Isaac Watts.

Jesus, Unchangeable and Unchanging.

The one true and living God is as the theologians say, immutable. In other words, He's unchangeable, being neither capable of nor susceptible to change. The Psalmist declares of God that, although everything is in a state of change, *"Thou art the same"* (Psalm 102:26-27). God remains the same throughout all eternity. He has the same will, character, plan, knowledge and wisdom as He has always had and always will have.

He has never remembered anything for there is nothing He has ever forgotten (except our sins). He cannot be taught, for He knows all things. He is forever constant and unchanging. He wants nothing, loses nothing and has no new thoughts. He is perfection and completion in all its unchangeable glory. There is, says James, no variableness or shadow of turning with him (James 1:17). We may change and say, *"I am not what I used to be,"* but God says, *"I am that I am'* (Exodus 3:14).

God, of a necessity, must be unchangeable otherwise He cannot be God. For example, if he can gain in power then He is not omnipotent. If He can gain knowledge and understanding, He is not omniscient. In short, one of the essential features of God is His immutability

--His unchangeableness. If it can be shown, therefore, that the Bible also attributes immutability to Christ Jesus then, once more, His deity is proven.

So, let us ask, did the writers of the New Testament know what they were talking about? Were they writing under the inspiration of the Holy Spirit or just making it up as they went along? Take note on how the Bible says in Psalm 102:26-27 that God is unchanging and immutable. How intriguing to notice that the writer to Hebrews quotes the same passage, but attributes it to Christ. He says;

"And, Thou, Lord, in the beginning hast laid the foundation of the earth; and the heavens are the works of your hands: They shall perish; but you remain; and they all shall wax old as does a garment;

And as a vesture shall you fold them up, and they shall be changed: but thou art the same, and thy years shall not fail (Hebrews 1:10-12).

The same, immutable God, who is unchanging in the Old Testament, is declared in the New Testament, to be none other than the Lord Jesus Christ. The only way, therefore, to avoid believing that Jesus is God is to believe that the Bible is not the Word of God. *"But surely God did change when He became human?"* Actually, He didn't! Remember this; Jesus has two natures, one human and one divine. His divine nature could not change.

His deity did not become human nor did his humanity become divine. Both His natures preserved their distinctive properties. He became a servant, but did not cease to be God. He made Himself of no reputation and veiled His deity: but at no time did He ever cease to be God. As R.C. Sproul says with his usual clarity,

"If God laid aside one of his attributes, the immutable undergoes a mutation, the infinite suddenly stops being infinite; it would be the end of the universe. God cannot stop being God and still be God. So we can't talk properly of God laying aside his deity to take humanity upon himself. That is why orthodox Christianity has always declared that Jesus was verus homus, verus Deus—truly man, truly God; fully man and fully God. His human nature was fully human, and his divine nature always and everywhere was fully divine.' R C Sproul: How Could Jesus Be Both Divine and Human?

Jesus Himself declared His immutability when He said; "*Heaven and earth shall pass away: but my words shall not pass away (Luke 21:33).* In order for His words not to pass away, they must be unchanging. Likewise, Christ Jesus will never change His mind about their truth. He will not amend, revise or update His words. They are unchangeable and full. Only an immutable person can speak words which will not develop, change or be abandoned throughout eternity. We worship the One who never changes: He is *Jesus Christ—the same yesterday today* and forever (Hebrews 13:8).

Chapter 4

So What's In A Name?

In John 17:26, when Jesus was praying, He said to the Father, "---*I have declared unto them thy name*". When Jesus claimed to have declared the name of God, he was saying He had made God both fully known and recognizable. As S.D. Gordon said, "Jesus is God spelling Himself out in language that men can understand."

The term '*name of God'* is intensely interesting. In Scripture, it stands for the divine perfections of God revealed in His character. We learn this in Exodus 33:18 when Moses was denied the request to see God's glory. However, God told Moses that, on the next day, He would proclaim His name to him. So on the following day, the LORD descended in the cloud, and stood with him there, and proclaimed the name of the LORD and said, ---"Hello there, my name is Fred!"

 No! That's not what He said, for that's not what He meant. When He said He would proclaim His name he wasn't talking about revealing some new moniker! When He said He would proclaim His name, He meant He would proclaim His divine perfections and character! Here's what He said; *And the LORD ----- stood with him there, and proclaimed the name of the LORD. And the LORD passed by before him, and proclaimed, The LORD, The LORD God, merciful and gracious, longsuffering, and abundant in goodness and truth, keeping mercy for thousands, forgiving iniquity and transgression and sin, and that will by no means clear the guilty;---- --" (Exodus 34:6-7).*

The name of God, therefore, reveals what God is like; it tells us about His character. This is what the psalmist means in Psalm 9:10 when He writes;

"And they that know thy name will put their trust in thee: for thou, LORD, hast not forsaken them that seek thee."

In other words, it is not whether or not we are on first name terms with God that makes the difference. It is, rather, when we know God's character (His name) we will be able to trust in Him because we will know what kind of God He is.

Furthermore, the name of God also stands for God Himself. Psalm 5:11 says,

"But let all those that put their trust in thee rejoice: let them ever shout for joy, because you defend them: let them also that love your name be joyful in you."

To love His name is to love God Himself. Consider also Psalm 20:1;

"---- the name of the God of Jacob defend thee;-- -"

This evidently means may God Himself defend you.

The Name of God sets before us, then, all that God has revealed about himself. Here are a few of the names of God. Each one of them tell us something about His character, and work. It is fascinating to see how Jesus revealed these names in His doing and dying, thus once more demonstrating that He is God.

God is known as Jehovah (Yahweh), the creator God in covenant with His redeemed people. Jehovah is the God who was and is and is to come. He is also known as,

Jehovah-Jireh, the LORD our Provider, Genesis 22:14.

Jehovah-Ropheka, the LORD our Healer, Exodus 15:26.

Jehovah -Shalom, the LORD our Peace, Judges 6:24.

Jehovah -Zidkenu, the LORD our Righteousness, Jeremiah 23:6, 33:16.

Jehovah- Roi, the LORD my Shepherd, Psalm 23:1.

Jehovah-Shammah, the LORD Ever Present, Ezekiel 48:35.

Did Jesus fulfil and declare these names? Was His life a manifestation of these names? Absolutely!

He is Jehovah Jireh, the Lord our Provider.

In Christ, we see Jehovah Jireh providing food for the mass of hungry people in the desert place (Matthew 14:19-20). And today, countless thousands of thousands of His followers know the reality of Jehovah Jireh as He meets all their daily needs.

But when this name Jehovah Jireh was first brought to our attention it had to do with substitutionary sacrifice. This event is found in Genesis 22 and it concerns the provision of a substitute for Isaac. Remember the story? The Lord had told His faithful friend Abraham to take his beloved son Isaac and sacrifice him on an altar. Old Abraham, I'm sure was confused and, if so, he had every right to be for, after all, the Lord had given him Isaac as a child of promise. Nevertheless, in obedience, the great man rose up early, took Isaac and journeyed to Mount Moriah. Remember how, as they climbed the mountain, Isaac turned to his father asking, "Where is the lamb?" and Abraham responded, "The Lord will provide Himself a lamb." Abraham knew that God would provide; he knew that God would see to it. He knew, by faith, that the Lord was Jehovah Jireh, the one who would provide a substitute for his boy. And indeed, God did provide a substitute and the place was then called Jehovah Jireh, 'the Lord has provided'.

We cannot leave this compelling story of Abraham and his boy without noticing that it is laced with gospel undertones. Notice that Abraham did not pray for a Lamb. He knew that God had seen the situation and that He would provide. Similarly, we didn't have to pray for God to send Christ to the cross to die for us. God knew and saw our need and in grace had already prepared the Lamb for the cross.

The wood was carried by Isaac points towards Christ carrying the cross up Mount Calvary. Isaac lying on the wood represented the Lord Jesus, who without a fight submitted to the Father's will. Look at Abraham's knife, it foreshadowed Jehovah's awful blade of justice falling upon Christ! Then consider the Ram! The ram was caught by the horns in some, thick, dense undergrowth comprised of interwoven thorny briars.

Being that horns are a picture of strength, we see that Christ's mighty power submitted itself to the hands of evil men, men whose sinful desires were woven together in the same manner as briers and thorns (see Micah 7:3). Thorns are also a by-product of the curse and the ram being imprisoned by them points towards Christ being made a curse for us (see Galatians 3:13).

Notice how the ram's head was entangled in the briars; this pictured how Christ's lovely head would be crowned with thorns.

That there are so many gospel pictures in this story, draws our attention to the fact that the greatest provision God has ever made was when He gave His own Son to be the wrath offering for our sins.

The God who is all-holy had demanded the sacrifice of Isaac. Isaac, like the rest of us, was a sinner and, therefore, deserved to die! That's a painful reality, but true! When Isaac asked the famous question, *"Where is the lamb"*, he didn't realize that the full answer to that question would not come for several thousand years. The answer would have to wait until the time when the hairy prophet stood upright on the banks of Jordan, pointed to the Lord Jesus and declared, *"Behold the Lamb of God."* It is as if he said, "This is the lamb about whom Isaac inquired and of whom Abraham prophesied!"

Jesus is the Lamb of God's preparation. Jesus is Jehovah Jireh the lamb of provision: Jesus in Himself is the provision for the sins of His people. He and only He is uniquely qualified for the title of, Jehovah-Jireh, the LORD our Provider! Once more Christ's deity is demonstrated.

Jesus is also Jehovah-Ropheka, the LORD our Healer.

In the Old Testament, Jehovah not only healed His people physically (Psalm 103:3), but also emotionally (Psalm 147:3). We must ask, therefore, did Jesus fully demonstrate and reveal God's character in this matter of healing? The answer is, of course, yes indeed He did. One of the characteristics of His ministry was that of healing. People flocked to Jesus to get healed. We read, *"and great multitudes followed him, and he healed them all"* (Matthew 12:15).

Did Jesus heal people emotionally? Yes indeed, He did. It was part of His ministry for He had been sent *"to heal the broken hearted, ----and to set at liberty those that are bruised"* (Luke 4:18).

Christ is the Great Physician: there never has been a healer or psychiatrist like Him for he "healed them all." I've known some people who genuinely seemed to have a gift of praying for the sick, but not one of them could say they had healed them all.

Some people went away just as sick as when they had arrived,---but when people came to Jesus, He healed them all. How did He do that? It was only possible because He was Jehovah-Ropheka in human flesh. So astonishing were His healings that His enemies characterized them as authored by the power of the devil (See Matthew 12: 22-29). He healed, deafness, blindness, disfigured bodies, withered hands, leprosy, paralysis, fever, and hemorrhages and raised the dead. Time after time, He demonstrated that He was Jehovah the healer. Indeed, each time He healed, He declared His identity as the self-existent Jehovah/Yahweh. How then do people say that Jesus never claimed to be God?

Is Jesus Jehovah -Shalom, the LORD our Peace?

Indeed He is! It was Jesus who said;

"Peace I leave with you, my peace I give unto you: not as the world gives, give I unto you. Let not your heart be troubled, neither let it be afraid" (John 14:27).

This wonderful name, Jehovah-Shalom, is first mentioned in Judges 6. There we discover Gideon, the unassuming and unsuspecting deliverer of his people. By the way, if ever there was a story of how God uses those who consider themselves to be unqualified for service it is this one. It seems, in those days, that just about anyone could invade Israel and help themselves to the crops. There was no resistance: Israel was, because of her sinful behaviour, rendered powerless to defend herself against any and all invading nations. It is thus in the midst of this scene that we find Gideon who, in a secret and clandestine effort to keep body and soul together, is secretly hiding his crops in the winepress.

Suddenly the pre-incarnate Christ appears as the Angel of the Lord and with perhaps a touch of humour greets him saying; *"The LORD is with thee thou mighty man of valour."* *"Who me? Yeah right,"* says Gideon, (and I paraphrase), *"If the LORD is so with me why am I having such a hard time from the Midianites, they are literally eating my lunch!*

Where are all the miracles that we heard about from our Fathers; where are the miracles that Jehovah did when he brought us up out of the land of Egypt? ---we could do with a few of us now!

This question was answered by a deafening silence. (We should note that no answer was given as a prophet had already come to Israel announcing why these calamities had happened (see verse 7). The Lord was not going to repeat Himself).

Then the Lord said;

"Go in this thy might, and you shall save Israel from the hand of the Midianites: have not I sent thee?

Gideon replies;

"Oh my Lord, how shall I save Israel? My family is poor in Manasseh, and I am the least in my father's house.

Gideon is disturbed: he is being asked to do something he cannot do in his own strength. However, assurances are given that the Lord will be with him. But still Gideon is distressed so he decides to put the matter to the test and asks if he can prepare a meal for the visitor. Permission is granted and when the meal is served Gideon is asked to place it on a rock and saturate it with broth. The heavenly visitor then stretches out his staff, touches the food, and flames consume the entire meal.

Gideon panics, and who can blame him? He realizes that he has seen God face to face and has lived! In grace, the Lord instantly alleviates his fears by speaking these wonderful words to him. 'Peace be unto thee; fear not: thou shalt not die." It was then that Gideon built an altar unto the LORD, and called it Jehovah-shalom, which means, Jehovah our peace!

Jehovah is our peace, there is no other! However, when we come to the New Testament we discover that it is Jesus Himself who is our peace! Ephesians 2:14 says," *For He* (Jesus) *is our peace.*" So let's ask then, is Jehovah- Shalom our peace or is Jesus our peace? If they are not one and the same then we have a problem. We have two rival identities vying to become 'our peace'. If Jehovah and Jesus are not one and the same then the Bible cannot be trusted.

Indeed people who say they believe the Bible, but who reject the Deity of Christ are actually declaring the Bible to be unreliable. They are left with two competing powers, one of whom is God and the other is a created being or a lesser God and each of them claiming to be our peace! As followers of Christ, however, we are called to embrace the One in whom all God's promises to us are fulfilled (2 Corinthians 1:20). We are to rest on the one who has paid every debt of sin we ever owed.

And in embracing the Lord Jesus, we embrace Jehovah- Shalom who is the very God of peace (Romans 16:20, Romans 15:33). So here again is the truth of the matter, if He's not God He's a fraud!

He is Jehovah -Zidkenu, The LORD our Righteousness, Jeremiah 23:6, 33:16.

This subject will be dealt with more fully in a later chapter, but in the meantime we must state that, in the New Testament, the Righteous One is Jesus Christ. When Peter was preaching in Acts 3:14 he declared, *"But you denied the Holy One and the Just (*The Righteous*), and desired a murderer to be granted unto you;*

When Paul was testifying in Acts 22:14 he said,

"The God of our fathers hath chosen you, that you should know his will, and see that Just One (The Righteous one), *and should hear the voice of his mouth.*

John teaches us,

"My little children, these things write I unto you, that ye sin not. And if any man sin, we have an advocate with the Father, Jesus Christ the righteous: (1 John 2:1). To be righteous means to fulfil all the demands placed upon us by virtue of being in covenant. Christ's whole life was one of righteousness.

By His life, and on our behalf, He fulfilled all the demands of the holiness of God. His people are now counted as righteous because of His holy obedience. This is the very essence of righteousness!

Furthermore, every promise God has made concerning man's salvation was kept in the person of Christ. God, therefore, fully demonstrated His righteousness through the Lord Jesus. Christ is, therefore, both the righteousness of man and the righteousness of God. Jesus is, therefore, Jehovah – Zidkenu the Lord our righteousness. If you say He's not God, you are saying He's a fraud!

Jesus is Jehovah- Roi (or Rohi), The LORD our Shepherd, Psalm 23:1

Jesus claims this title for Himself saying He is the *'Good Shepherd'* (John 10:11). In the New Testament,

He is also spoken of as the *great Shepherd* (Hebrews 13:20), the *chief Shepherd* (1 Peter 5:4) and the *Shepherd and bishop of our souls, (1 Peter 2:25)*. As our shepherd, He cares for and protects every believer on an ongoing, daily basis.

While on earth the great Shepherd cared for His little flock. As a shepherd He prayed continually for them. Remember in Luke 22:31-32 we read how Jesus said,

" Simon, Simon, behold, Satan hath desired to have you, that he may sift you as wheat: But I have prayed for thee, that thy faith fail not:"

This is excellent shepherding! In effect, Jesus says, "Simon, Satan hatched a plot to get you, but I got there first: I've already prayed for you!"

Another thing about a shepherd and his sheep is that, although sheep are not the most intelligent of creatures, they know the voice of their shepherd. Jesus demonstrated that He was Jehovah the Shepherd by walking into places where 'his sheep' worked and calling them to follow Him. Matthew, for example, was hard at work collecting taxes and Jesus walked straight up to him commanding him to follow. Matthew heard the voice of the Shepherd and left everything behind him (Matthew 9:9). The only thing he took with him, perhaps, was his pen, a thing he put to excellent use in later days!

Also, as a Shepherd, Jesus lost none of His sheep. This ability is again a declaration of His Deity. Listen to Jesus as He prays,

"While I was with them in the world, I kept them in thy name: those that thou gave me I have kept, and none of them is lost, but the son of perdition; that the scripture might be fulfilled (John 17:12).

Jesus, the Good Shepherd, has never lost a sheep. By doing so, He fully demonstrates that He is the divine shepherd of Psalm 80. Concerning this divine shepherd we read;

"Let thy hand be upon the man of thy right hand, upon the son of man whom thou made strong for thyself. So will not we go back from thee: (see Psalm 80:17-19).

The work of the Divine Shepherd is to ensure that His people do not turn away from Him. This is exactly what Jesus claimed He had done in John 17 and through this claim once more demonstrated Himself to be God in human flesh.

Furthermore, it is written that Yahweh as a Judge was to scatter Israel, but as a Shepherd He would gather the sheep and keep them (Jeremiah 31:10). Again the Lord Jesus Christ in John 17 claims this same keeping power of the Almighty. If He's not God, He's a fraud!

Jesus has declared Jehovah's name in this matter of shepherding. He has visibly and powerfully demonstrated what God the Shepherd is like. Neither you nor I could do this, nor could any human being on the face of this earth accomplish this; but Jesus is able to do this because He is God manifest in the flesh.

Jehovah-Shammah, the LORD Ever Present, Ezekiel 48:35.

Jesus claimed this title for Himself when he sent the disciples out to evangelize the world. He said, "Go ye therefore, and teach all nations, ------- and, lo, I am with you always, even unto the end of the world (Matthew 28:19-20). To be enabled to fulfil His promise to be with His people in all places at the same time He would have to be Jehovah-Shammah. No mere man could send people to various parts of the globe and promise to be with every one of them at all times. If He's not God, He's a fraud! So what's in a name? Everything, when it comes to God. Listen again to what Jesus said to the Father,

"And I have declared unto them thy name" (John 17:26).

Jesus revealed the name (the divine character) of God perfectly------an impossible thing for a mere mortal to do. To do such a thing, He had to be the visible image of the invisible God. Jesus, our Saviour, has made God fully known. He has declared His name. The riches and glory of the gospel is that the name of the covenant God of Israel, the strong and mighty Yahweh, has been unfolded and declared in and by Jesus Christ. Jesus is the perfect representative and representation of God. He is the image of the invisible God.

As we've already noticed, Jesus took the guesswork out of God. We no longer have to sit and wonder what The Father is like. The Father has come to us in the person of His Son and revealed Himself to us. He has spelt Himself out to us in words and actions we can grasp. Let Muslims and JWs and others who are cut from the same cloth reject this marvellous truth if they will: however, if they reject that Christ Jesus is God, then they count themselves unworthy of salvation. They have rejected He who is 'The Way'. Before we move on we need to say that Jesus is not a way that leads to the Way.

He is 'The Way'. He is the way to the Father's presence and the way to the Father's person. He has declared His name. Only God himself can make such a declaration and that is why Jesus was able to confidently say in John 17:26, "*I have declared unto them thy name.*"

Sovereign Divine Power Demonstrated In the Name of Jesus.

In Luke 10:17, seventy enthusiastic disciples returned from their preaching mission. I can just hear the awe and wonder in their voices as they report to the Master that the very demons were subject to them when they used His name. It is no wonder that they were gripped with amazement. They knew that the demons were, after all, under the direct authority of Satan (Beelzebub the ruler of the demons---see Matthew 12:24).

Satan is called by many names in Scripture among which are;

The Dragon (Isaiah 27:1; Revelation 20:2);

The Enemy (Matthew 13:39);

The Father of lies (John 8:44);

A great red dragon (Revelation 12:3);

That old serpent (Revelation12:9; 20:2);

The Power of darkness (Colossians 1:13);

The Prince of this world (John 14:30);

The Prince of the power of the air (Ephesians 2:2);

The Ruler of the darkness of this world (Ephesians 6:12);

The Spirit that works in the children of disobedience (Ephesians 2:2);

The god of this world (2 Corinthians 4:4);

The Wicked one (Matthew 13:19,38);

What an array of titles! And these are only but some! Now here's a question for those who say that Jesus was merely a man. How can the name of a mere man topple the hordes of demonic powers controlled by the prince and god of this world? Yet the name of Jesus routed the legions of demonic armies. The name of Alexander or Caesar would not have moved them, but time and time again the demons lost all control when confronted by the name of Jesus the Christ. Of course we see the Lord Jesus Himself taking authority over the devils and this, in and of itself, points towards His deity. But in Luke 10, He sends out the disciples, armed only with His name, and the demons fall. Just try sending someone out to make demons fall in your name! It won't work!

The devils will just look at your messenger and perhaps attack him as they did the unfortunate sons of Sceva (Acts 19: 16).

What immense power, therefore, is bound up in this wonderful name of the Lord Jesus Christ! Luther writes,

"I, out of my own experience, am able to witness, that Jesus Christ is true God; I know full well and have found what the name of Jesus has done for me. I have often been so near death, that I thought verily now must I die, because I teach his Word to the wicked world, and acknowledge him; but always he mercifully put life into me, refreshed and comforted me.'   Martin Luther: The Smalcald Articles.

There is no other name like the name of Jesus! In Luke 24:47 we are told repentance and forgiveness of sins should be preached in Jesus' name.

In John 1:12, authority is given to become God's children, because of faith in Jesus' name.

In Acts 10:43 everyone putting faith in Jesus receives forgiveness of sins through his name.

In Acts 4:12 we discover that there is no other name under heaven by which we must be saved.

In John 14:13-14, 26 we are told that whatever we ask, He will do, if we ask in Jesus' name.

In Acts 3:16 a man was made strong through faith in Jesus' name.

In Acts 4:7-10, 30 healing and signs came in Jesus' name.

In Ephesians 1:21 Jesus' name is far above every name named.

In Philippians 2:9-11, every knee shall bow at Jesus' name.

In Revelation 1:6, 5:9 the worship of the redeemed is drawn out at the mere mention of Jesus' name.

So how say you then that He is merely a man? What name can do all of this? What name has done more good for more people throughout the ages than the name of Jesus? Bishop Ryle astutely observes;

"Jesus is a name, which is peculiarly sweet and precious to believers. It has often done them good, when the favour of kings and princes would have been heard of with unconcern. It has given them what money cannot buy, even inward peace. It has eased their wearied consciences, and given rest to their heavy hearts. The Song of Solomon speaks the experience of many, when it says, "your name is oil poured forth." (Song of Solomon 1:3.)

Happy is that person, who trusts not merely in vague notions of God's mercy and goodness, but in "Jesus." Bishop Ryle, Gospel of Matthew.

His Name, Jesus

"----thou shalt call His name Jesus for he shall save his people from their sins. Matthew 1:21.

"He saves them from the guilt of sin, by washing them in His own atoning blood. He saves them from the dominion of sin, by putting in their hearts the sanctifying Spirit. He saves them from the presence of sin, when He takes them out of this world to rest with Him. He will save them from all the consequences of sin, when He shall give them a glorious body at the last day. Blessed and holy are Christ's people! From sorrow, cross, and conflict they are not saved. But they are saved from sin for evermore. They are cleansed from guilt by Christ's blood.   J.C. Ryle: Commentary on Matthew.

Matthew 1:21 is both a promise and a prophesy. It says,*"Thou shalt call his name JESUS, for he shall save his people from their sins."* Notice how Jesus was prophetically named for His name was a prophesy concerning His future work. This child would grow up and save His people from their sins by one great redemptive act; therefore, the prophetic word is bound up in the very name of Jesus. But His name is not only a prophesy, it is also a promise to all of us who are so ruined that we know we cannot save ourselves.

Listen again as the angel says, *"He shall save."* This is a magnificent promise. If He shall and will save us, then we should abandon all our silly efforts to save ourselves!

But what has this to do with His deity? Notice again how His parents were to *"Call his name Jesus."* This name is the Greek equivalent of the Hebrew name Joshua which means "Jehovah or Yahweh, our Saviour." So once more we are confronted by another proof of His deity. He is Yahweh our Saviour!

Of course, the name Jesus was a common name in those days. Obviously people who bore that name were not the LORD incarnate. Obviously, for example, General Joshua of the Old Testament was not God incarnate nor was he Jehovah the Saviour. But when we read of the naming of Jesus we are confronted immediately by the truth that He is Yahweh, God manifest in the flesh. So what's the difference? Why is Jesus God, but Joshua a mere man?

Good question! To answer it, let's look at the text and ask why it is we are to call Him Jesus Yahweh the Saviour. As we read the text, we discover we are to call Him this because He shall save his people from their sins! Now let me remind you, salvation is the work of Yahweh alone. But, since Jesus accomplished salvation, we must conclude that by doing so, He declared His true identity and demonstrates that He is Yahweh the Saviour! Since it is the unique function of Yahweh to save His people and since the Lord Jesus equally has this same distinctive function, we again conclude that Christ and Yahweh are one and the same! Jesus is God! If, however, Jesus does not save His people, He is not Yahweh.

Indeed, the cults such as the JWs declare that, yes Jesus saves his people (albeit with our good works thrown in for good measure). In spite of this admission, they do not connect the dots for they maintain that, even though he saves, He is not Yahweh.

So what about those other children called Jesus or Joshua in those days? Were they also Jehovah in human flesh? No! They were called 'Jesus' by their parents. The difference between them and the Master was that Jesus was named by the Father. It was by God's direct instructions that Christ was to be named Jesus. Often in Scripture, when God names someone He identifies them as who they really are.

Consider that God has called (named) all believers sons of God (1 John 3:1). The reason we are called this is that we are actually and really Sons of God. Again, we see that God changed the name of Jacob, whose name meant 'supplanter', to Israel,

which means 'one who rules with God'. This is who he actually had become and God called him accordingly.

When God named a person, His naming of them decreed what they were and what they would do. Thus the Master was named Jesus. In effect, the angel said, "Call him Yahweh Saves, for He shall save His people from their sins."

Furthermore, it is interesting to note that our Lord was called by a Greek name, Jesus, and not a Hebrew one. I suspect, although many would not agree, this is not merely a translation for our convenience. I suspect, along with others, that He never was called Joshua or Jeheshua; Most likely He was always known as "Jesus" for this was the name put upon the inscription attached to the cross: It read, "This is Jesus, (not Jeheshua) the king of the Jews." It is not hard to believe that He was always called Jesus, a Gentile name, because it would indicate that "his People" had reference to much more than the Jewish people. His people would come from all the nations of the earth.

Dearest of all the names above,
My Jesus, and my God,
Who can resist Thy heav'nly love,
Or trifle with Thy blood?

'Tis by the merits of Thy death
The Father smiles again;
'Tis by Thine interceding breath
The Spirit dwells with men.

But if Immanuel's face appear,
My hope, my joy begins;
His Name forbids my slavish fear,
His grace removes my sins.

Isaac Watts

In conclusion, the Lord is named Jesus, which means Yahweh the Saviour, thus again, in Him alone, we see God and man in one person. Furthermore, this child will be not merely "Yahweh a Saviour" for He is much more; He is "Yahweh our Saviour"; "Yahweh our deliverer"; the one through whom our sins and iniquities have been taken away.

 So remember, every time we call on this wonderful name of Jesus, we are affirming our belief that He is the mighty God!

If you don't believe He is God, don't call Him Jesus for, if He's not God, He's a fraud. The Father, however, named Him Jesus to establish that He was to be the God/Man. If you reject His identity, you have deprived yourself of access to the most wonderful name in Heaven and on earth. Furthermore, if you reject that He is God, and yet call Him Jesus, you are flying in the very face of the Almighty!

His Name, Emmanuel

"Veiled in flesh the Godhead see;
Hail th' Incarnate Deity,
Pleased as man with man to dwell;
Jesus, our Emmanuel."

"And they shall call His name Emmanuel which being interpreted is God with us."

Matthew 1:23.

His name is Emmanuel; what a giveaway! Even a headless man on a galloping horse can see this one. This verse tells us two things. First, Jesus is God and second, as God, He is with us. He is called Emmanuel, a Hebrew name which when translated means, "God with us." He is God with and amongst us; He is God as one of us; He is God, as a human, involved with humanity.

Jesus was and is truly God. It would indeed be impossible for Jesus our Emmanuel not to be God for His name is a revelation of His omnipresence---He is with us. We've already touched on His omnipresence, but think about it again, for Him to be 'with us' He has to be omnipresent: if He is not omnipresent He cannot be with all of us at the same time --- that's a no-brainer! If He was a mere man and not omnipresent, He can be with me, but if He is with me then He is not with you and vice versa.

But we are to call Him Emmanuel for He is God with all of us. He is the God who is everywhere present at all times. I don't suppose the cults like to call him Emmanuel for they dare not admit His omnipresence, and thus His Deity.

But In the Old Testament, 800 years before Jesus was born, the prophet Isaiah foretold His birth, saying, *"Behold a virgin shall conceive, and bear a son, and they shall call his name Immanuel" (Isaiah 7:13-14).* I suppose the cults must think that poor old Isaiah was wrong on this one! After all, if Jesus is not God then He is not Emmanuel! If, however, the cults actually believe what they teach they will have to tear Isaiah from their Bibles for he dared to tell us that the Virgin's child would be Emmanuel.

Not only so, but they must also shred Matthew from their Bibles as he concurs with Isaiah's deception! It was, after all, Matthew who said,

"Now all this was done, that it might be fulfilled which was spoken of the Lord by the prophet, saying, Behold, a virgin shall be with child, and shall bring forth a son, and they shall call his name Emmanuel, which being interpreted is, God with us" (Matthew 1:22-23).

If the cults who deny Christ's deity are correct, both Matthew and Isaiah are unreliable. They should shun them, but they don't.

However, the Scripture plainly says, "They shall call his name Emmanuel" No ifs, ands or buts-- call Him Emmanuel-God with us! But, have you ever noticed anyone in the New Testament calling Him by this name? I haven't! Can this verse then be a mistake? For our answer, we should remember what, *"To be called"* actually means. We mentioned this in the last section on "His Name: Jesus." Wesley, gives us further insight into this when he writes; "To be called, means, according to the Hebrews manner of speaking, that the person spoken of shall really and effectually be what he is called, and actually fulfil that title. Thus, Unto us a child is born - and his name shall be called Wonderful, Counsellor the Mighty God, the Prince of Peace - That is, he shall be all these, though not so much nominally, as really, and in effect. And thus was he called Emmanuel; which was no common name of Christ, but points out his nature and office; as he is God incarnate, and dwells by his Spirit in the hearts of his people." Wesley's Notes.

What a Saviour we have!

Jesus Christ, the almighty King of kings and Lord of lords, stooped to become an infant and, as Emmanuel, came here to be God with us!

What immense condescension! Look and see His young teenage mother sustaining the sustainer of all things! There He is, in the stable, dependent and vulnerable yet, at the same time as He is guarded by His parents, He is guarding them as He upholds all things by the word of his power. Does this not call out a spirit of worship from His people? Think of it, God in a feeding trough for cattle! There He is, a baby, lying there with no human Father and no divine Mother. He's wonderful!

 God is with us! If you are one of His, call Him who He is, the incarnate God, Emmanuel. Bishop Ryle with his usual insightfulness writes,

"Would you have a strong foundation for your faith and hope? Then keep in constant view your Saviour's divinity. He in whose blood you are taught to trust is the Almighty God. All power is His in heaven and earth. None can pluck you out of His hand. If you are a true believer in Jesus, let not your heart be troubled or afraid."   J.C Ryle: Commentary on Matthew.

But, did Jesus really believe He was Emmanuel, God with us? He most certainly did! This is why He told his disciples, *"Lo I am with you always even unto the end of the world"* (Matthew 28: 20). Since repetition is the price of learning, let's again remember that He claimed He would be with each of the disciples wherever they went and was, therefore, making a declaration of His omnipresence. Was Jesus mistaken about this matter? If so, the man was a fool and unsuitable material from which to build a Saviour for the world! Was Jesus delusional? To claim omnipresence is to claim an essential quality belonging exclusively to God. Jesus by this one claiming this was declaring Himself the master of both space and time. Is this the kind of thing we can excuse if it is not true? If this is a lie that Jesus is telling, then run away from Him---He's not the Way, He's not the Truth ---He's not the Answer! But, if that which Jesus is saying is true, worship him, lay down your life for Him, trust Him, love Him serve Him and follow Him.

Furthermore, consider this: Have you ever noticed how that in the Old Testament, Yahweh comforted His people with the very words "I am with you"?

Moses, Joshua and Jeremiah all heard these wonderful words. But now in the New Testament, it is the Lord Jesus who gives this promise to His followers. Jesus has, in effect, stepped into the place of Yahweh by employing Yahweh's exact language. Does it not cause your heart to worship? It should do, for Jesus Himself is wonderful! He is God, in flesh, appearing! Watts captured some of the wonder of the eternal God stooping to be with us when he penned the lines,

"Archangels leave their high abode

To learn new mysteries here, and tell

The loves of our descending God,

The glories of Emmanuel."

Isaac Watts: 1674-1748.

Those of us who follow Him, know He is Emmanuel: He is with us wherever we are. He is our guide and sustainer! He is with us because He is God, and God is omnipresent. There is no such thing as an omnipresent angel; even Satan is not omnipresent.

This then begs the question as to how those so-professed Christians who deny His deity can call upon Him in times of trouble. How do they find Him? Does He have to rush to their aid from some distant domain? At what speed does He travel? They must consider that, if He is not God, He is not omnipresent. If, however, they believe that Christ will never leave them and that He is with them at all times, they must admit that He is Omnipresent and must, therefore, also acknowledge that He is God. They can't have it both ways!

Those of us, however, who believe in His Deity, have no difficulty in embracing a Saviour who is not only seated in Majesty in Heaven, but who is also our constant companion, helper and strength. Jesus is the Lord Ever-Present, He is Emmanuel, God with us.

His Name, the Mediator

Hebrews 12:24; 'Jesus the mediator of the new covenant.'

"There cannot be any point of contact between absolute deity and fallen humanity except through Jesus Christ, the appointed Mediator. That is God's door: all else is a wall of fire. You can by Christ approach the Lord, but this is the sole bridge across the gulf." Spurgeon: Peace: A Fact and a Feeling: Sermon #1456.

Between the all-holy God and sin-filled man there stands the stunning, sinless person of the Lord Jesus Christ. The genius of the gospel is that Christ is Himself both God and man and thus is a fitting and qualified mediator between us both. In Christ, man encounters the all-holy God and in Christ, God encounters the perfect man. Jesus, therefore, because He is both God and man, is the only one exclusively qualified to be our mediator. Indeed, He must be both God and man to qualify as an effective representative of both parties. If He were merely man He could not represent God: If God only, He could not represent man.

So what is a mediator? The services of mediators are often employed to help resolve business disputes. There are perceived offences on both sides, and the mediator carefully guides the warring parties through the troubled waters till at last a settlement of peace is reached.

Of course, this picture breaks down when applied to the dispute between God and man. We alone have caused the breach. We are the offending party. God is entirely innocent of any suggested crimes and utterly filled with integrity in His dealings with us. We are the errant faction.

So let's be clear on this, Christ is the only qualified mediator because He is both God and man. He fully represents us to God and fully represents God to us. He is the meeting place between God and man. If we will not meet with God in Christ, we will not meet with God at all until that final and dreadful Day of Judgment. If a man will not meet with God through the appointed mediator, then he will have no advocate or lawyer to defend Him against the record of sin that was his life.

I would remind you that our hope of salvation rests in Christ alone. If He does not save us, then we will not be saved. If His blood has not paid the ransom and does not mediate for us, right now, then we are lost and sold under sin. The gospel has inseparably bound us to Christ, our Lord and Saviour.

But what if He is, as some say, not God? If He is not God, we are in serious trouble! Let's say, for example, that Jesus is the highest exalted angel in existence, but not God, what then would happen to us if Jesus and God argued and fell out? What if they fought and God banished Jesus from Heaven? That would be disastrous for us because if He gets banished then we get banished! If He is unaccepted, then we are unaccepted. If that shocks you, then perhaps you need to revisit your understanding of the gospel. Listen to the truth of this scripture,

"God has <u>for Christ's sake</u> forgiven us" (Ephesians 4:32).

We are not forgiven because we turned over a new leaf and became good. We are forgiven for Christ's sake alone.

We are *Chosen in Christ* (Ephesians 1:4). In other words, we were not chosen in ourselves or because of anything to do with us, our election is 'in Christ'!

Furthermore, it is, *'in Christ Jesus'* that we have redemption (Ephesians 1:7) and, in addition, we are accepted only in Christ the Beloved One (Ephesians 1:6). We must remember that we are saved only by His work, a work done for us and done as us, yet done apart from us. He represents us in Heaven, and we are clothed in His righteousness alone.

If His work for us is entirely wrong, then we are entirely wrong! It is Christ and His doing and dying alone that qualify us to be in Glory. He guarantees our welcome and thus it is of a necessity that he is God.So, if Jesus is not God, then none of us who have trusted Him are actually safe. We will only be safe as long as Jesus and God don't fall out! We are only secure as long as there is no disagreement between Christ Jesus and God. My favour and acceptance with God are not bound up with anything to do with me---it has all to do with Jesus Christ.

And before you say, *"Oh well such a thing could not happen, Jesus and God could not fall out and disagree,"* I would like to remind you that the highest created angel, the onetime Prince in Heaven, Mr. Lucifer, fell out with God and was cast out of glory. So what's to stop the same thing happening with and to Jesus? It is not actually beyond the realm of possibility, if Jesus is merely a created being. Let's say it again, if Jesus is not God then there is an actual risk, be it ever so slight, that God and Jesus will, sometime down the line, not see eye to eye, we, then, in that eventuality, will be lost. We, therefore, must face the fact that none of us is actually and permanently reconciled to God. Reconciliation with the Father is a mere fiction if we can potentially be thrown out of Heaven. So much for the verse that teaches we are reconciled to God by the death of Christ (Romans 5:10)! It's a mere fantasy

and a vain imagination. So much for preaching the message of reconciliation (2 Corinthians 5:20)! Reconciliation by Christ is an empty promise if Christ is not God. Furthermore, if Christ is not God then the Bible is unreliable for it makes promises upon.

In addition, think about this; if Jesus is not God, we don't have to wait for eternity to be disadvantaged! What about this life? We all need a compassionate and all-powerful High priest to get us through each day.

We need a priest who is able to save us to the uttermost (Hebrews 7:25); we need a priest who is able to, continually, present us faultless (Jude 1:24); we need a priest who is, continually, able to keep us from falling (Jude 1:24) and, continually, able to help us when we are tempted (Hebrews 2:18). But, how can a mere man or created being do all that for us? If Jesus is not God, then He is quite useless as a mediator and High Priest. The kind of priest we need is one who can hear all of his people's prayers at all times. He has to know us and be able to search our hearts. A mere man could not do all of this. which God may not deliver. Only the God/Man can, therefore, be qualified to become our faithful, effective mediator and High Priest. But Christ is God and, since God cannot fall out with Himself, we are saved, secure, reconciled and safe. This is Good News: this is gospel truth; in fact there is no gospel, no good news, if Jesus is not God!

For Christ to be the mediator, he must be fully God and fully man! No other mediator is suitable for both parties.

Reject Him as God and you have no mediator. If He is a mere man, or an angel, we have no mediator. If He understands one side, but not the other, He is inept, and His judgment flawed.

Therefore, only in Christ Jesus do we have the provision of a qualified mediator. What comfort there is in knowing this wonderful truth! As Isaac Watts said,

O joy there sitteth in our flesh

Upon a throne of light

One of human mother born

In perfect Godhead bright.

His Name, The LORD.

When we call him Lord, we are declaring that He is the Sovereign. When we call Him Jesus, we are declaring that He is the Saviour, and when we call Him Christ, we are declaring that He is the Sufficient One. He is the Sufficient, Sovereign Saviour! This is a remarkable combination of saving power and wisdom. And yet there are those that refuse to see that only a Sufficient, Sovereign Saviour can possibly be God. Let's now look at the word 'LORD' more closely. To say that someone is 'LORD', is to admit that they are the one in charge. Jesus continually demonstrated His Lordship and sovereignty over all things, thus proving continually that He was God.

He was Lord over all nature and with a single word calmed a storm. He demonstrated that He was Lord over death by raising the dead. He demonstrated His sovereignty over Satan each time He cast out demons. Sovereignty is God's domain! Is it any wonder then that Jesus gave an uninterrupted demonstration that He possessed it?

Yet, when God showed up in the person of Jesus, He was rejected and scorned. In fact, men's hatred boiled against him. But, in the midst of this hatred, Christ took wonderful opportunities to demonstrate His sovereignty. Do you remember when one Sabbath the church people got so mad at His sermon that they decided to kill him? In their fury, they marched Him to the edge of the cliff to hurl Him off, but Jesus decided He wasn't going to die that day and simply walked away (Luke 4:28-30). No one stopped Him; no one laid a finger on Him. I can just imagine afterwards someone asking, "How did He do that?" To turn and walk through a crowd that is in the very act of trying to murder you is Sovereignty. In His Sovereignty, Jesus chose the manner of His death; He chose the cross and refused to be killed by a mob. That's the mark of God. He not only chose the manner of His death.

He chose the precise moment of His death. When He was satisfied that redemption had been accomplished, He bowed His head and dismissed His Spirit. He was entirely Sovereign over the very second of His death.

Only God can do that. Dying is not as easy as you think! Of course, you can choose the moment of your death by shooting yourself, but apart from that, just try dying --right this second --- just will to die right now! You can't do it! No one can, for we do not have that kind of authority or power. Power such as that is reserved for the One who alone is Sovereign. The Greek word for Lord is '*Kurios*' and means 'Supreme Authority'. This is the word that was continually used to translate the Tetragrammaton (a four-letter Hebrew name) which stood for the name of Yahweh in the Greek translation of the Old Testament (the Septuagint). The early Christians, knowing the usage of this word Kurios, refused, therefore, to swear an oath of allegiance to the Roman Emperor. And what was the oath? They were required to declare, "Caesar is the Kurios" which meant, "Caesar is the Lord." Along with the oath they were also required to burn incense to the Emperor's image. The Roman state saw this as an affirmation of political loyalty, but the Christians saw it quite differently. They saw this as an idolatrous act that betrayed Christ.

In their enlightened understanding, there was only one Kurios --- Jesus! There could be only one supreme authority. Since there is no authority higher than that which is supreme, the Christians knew that to declare the Emperor the Kurios would be to declare him as God. They, therefore, refused to do so and paid with their lives.

There are those who point out that the term 'kurios' could have been used of anyone in a position of authority. It could, in fact, refer to anyone who was a leader. Property owners were called "Lord" (Matthew 20:8). Heads of households were called "Lord" (Mark 13:35). Slave owners were called "Lord" (Matthew 10:24). Husbands were called "Lord" (1 Peter 3:6). This is true, but when the apostles used the term Lord they were declaring Jesus to be much more than a leader, property owner or head of a household;

They were declaring Him to be God. They weren't killed for refusing to declare Caesar as the head of his household, they were killed for refusing to call the emperor God. Jesus was their God, there was room for no other. The apostles urged their listeners to call upon the name of the Lord, the mighty God, the sovereign, supreme authority.

In Romans 10:9, Paul declared, *"if you confess with your mouth the Lord Jesus... you shall be saved."*

Then in Romans 10:13, Paul backs up this declaration by quoting from the Old Testament,

"For whoever will call upon the name of the LORD shall be delivered (saved)" (Joel 2:32).

It is remarkable to note that when Joel 2:32 is quoted in both Acts 2:21 and Romans 10:13, the "LORD" in question is identified as Jesus. This is all the more significant when we remember that the Jewish faith had always taught that the people should call upon the name of Yahweh.

Consider this, among other things, the Israelites were to call upon Yahweh in prayer;

"I have called upon thee, for thou wilt hear me, O God: incline thine ear unto me, and hear my speech. "Psalm 17:6.

Yahweh was to be called upon for deliverance (salvation);

Psalm 116:4 *"Then called I upon the name of the LORD; O LORD, I beseech thee, deliver my soul."*

Yahweh was to be called upon for help;

Lamentations 3:55 *"I called upon thy name, O LORD, out of the low dungeon."*

But when we reach the pages of the New Testament, we see Jewish Christians insisting that people should no longer call on Yahweh, the Old Testament name of God, but now they must call only on the name of Jesus: Their conviction concerning Jesus was, "there is no other name under heaven given to men by which we must be saved" Acts 4:12.

The early Christian, most of whom were Jewish, were persuaded that to call Jesus Lord was to call him Yahweh. This being so, we should inform the cults that, in reality, they cannot make the confession, "Jesus is Lord" because these three words are a confession of Christ's supreme deity!

For the early Jews, being confronted by the confession of the Lordship of Christ was something greater than acknowledging Jesus as a leader or property owner. It was a confession that the Sovereign God of the Old Testament had visited the earth and had walked among them. This same Jesus with whom they had eaten and shared daily life was none other than the eternal Yahweh! We cannot over-emphasize this: The people of Israel were raised on scriptures such as,

Psalm 18:3, "I will call upon the LORD, who is worthy to be praised: so shall I be saved from mine enemies."

Psalm 55:16, "As for me, I will call upon God; and the LORD shall save me."

Psalm 86:15, "For thou, Lord, art good, and ready to forgive; and plenteous in mercy unto all them that call upon thee."

Psalm 116:2, "I will call upon him (Yahweh) as long as I live."

Psalm 116: 13, "I will take the cup of Salvation and call upon the name of the Lord."

 Now all Israel is being told to call upon the name of Jesus. Jesus is the Lord upon whom they are to call. This is make or break time! Commands like this cannot be greeted with neutrality. If Jesus is the God of the Old Testament, then call Him LORD. If he is not,

call Him teacher, the son of David or a prophet, but don't call Him LORD. If He's not God, He's a fraud!

Since; however, Jesus is God, Christians freely call Him Lord. In 1 Corinthians 12: 3 we read,

"No man can say that Jesus is the Lord but by the Holy Ghost."

To recite the words, "Jesus is Lord", means little; but to say them with heart belief that He is Yahweh takes a work of the Spirit.

Someone once said that, He listens to our words with a stethoscope. He knows what's in our hearts. So, what say you? Is He Lord? If He is, then He is your God! Do not, therefore, be ashamed to confess Him as such!

His Name, King of kings and Lord of Lords.

Related to the truth of His divine lordship and sovereignty is His title, the King of kings. We read in Revelation 17:14,

"These shall make war with the Lamb, and the Lamb shall overcome them: for He is Lord of lords, and King of kings:

And in Revelation 19:16 we read;

"And he hath on His vesture and on his thigh a name written, KING OF KINGS, AND LORD OF LORDS."

That He is Lord of all lords is again a declaration of His deity. In the Old Testament, it is Yahweh who is given the title Lord of Lords. We read, *"For the LORD your God is God of gods and Lord of lords, a great God, mighty and terrible, who regards not persons nor take reward no partiality nor takes a bribe"* (Deuteronomy 10:17).

Ascribing the title *'Lord of lords'* to the Lord Jesus is, therefore, no small matter. It proves once more that the Bible declares Him to be God!

Also, this title, King of Kings, as found in Revelation 17:14, once more demonstrates that Christ Jesus is fully God and fully man. As the Lamb, He has supreme dominion and power over all things; all the kings

of the earth are subject to His control and rulership. A crown of royal rulership has replaced His crown of thorns.

The Puritan, Thomas Manton, gives wonderful insight into this title King of Kings when He says; "He that was to be King of kings and Lord of lords needed to be both God and man. God, that he might cast out the prince of this world,

and having rescued his church from the power of darkness, might govern it by his word and Spirit, and finally present it to himself a glorious church, without spot or wrinkle, or any such thing.

Thomas Manton: Sermon 7 on Colossians 1: 14-20: Volume 1 of Manton's works.

Christ is the King of kings and the Lord of lords. In Him, the invisible King has become visible and has been perfectly expressed:

His wisdom, His will, His excellences, His sovereign authority are now seen clearly in the Lord Jesus Christ. Let whomever among us who wants to know God's power, majesty and glory, look to Christ and to Christ alone.

"Jesus, the Saviour, reigns, the God of truth and love;
When He had purged our stains He took His seat above;
Lift up your heart, lift up your voice;
Rejoice, again I say, rejoice!"

His Name: The Amen.

When we say, "Amen" as someone prays, we are saying, "So let it be." By adding our 'Amen', we are simply adding our agreement to the prayer. When God says, 'Amen'; however, He is saying, "And so it shall be." He is the God of truth and faithfulness, and when He says that something will happen, the very fact that He has said it confirms the matter. God is the guarantor of His word.

He is the One who cannot lie; He is the one with the power necessary to bring His word to pass. That which God declares, will indeed, come to pass because He is faithful, powerful and reliable.

The root meaning of 'Amen' from Hebrew has to do with faithfulness and includes the ideas of nourishing, making strong and truth. Amen came to be associated with a solemn declaration by God or an agreement with the truth of God. In fact, God is designated, in Isaiah 65:16, as "the God of truth," literally, "the God of Amen." It is of no surprise, then, that Jesus used the "double amen or 'verily, verily' throughout the gospel of John. Remember how He said to Nicodemus, "Verily, verily I say unto you except a man be born again he cannot see the Kingdom of God."

Literally, what Jesus said was, "Amen, Amen, I say unto you." Charles Alexander says, "It must have struck

Nicodemus like a thunderbolt to hear the Saviour declare (with all the solemnity of one speaking from the throne of God,) "Amen, amen, I say unto thee, except a man be born again he cannot see the kingdom of God."

Charles Alexander, The Spiritual Application of John's Gospel: Chapter 7.

He further states that, "John is the only gospel writer to use the double "verily" or "amen", He uses it with great frequency. The double Amen declares that the one who speaks is Himself the Amen, the conclusion of all things, the only truth, the possessor of all wisdom, the full and final authority who speaks

from above'

Ibid.

Notice how Jesus reversed the accepted order of speech. Most people use the word 'amen' at the end of a sentence, but Christ uses it at the very beginning. He is the Alpha and Omega of divine revelation being that He is both the beginning and the end of the revelation of God. He is the Amen of the will of God, the one who fulfilled the eternal purposes perfectly and entirely. It is in Christ Jesus that we see the faithful fulfillment of the promises of God.

Beginning with Genesis 3:15, God promised the defeat of the serpent (Satan) by the seed of the woman. Through successive generations, many additional promises were given concerning the coming seed, the great deliverer of the people of God. Now in Christ, these promises have been faithfully fulfilled. He is the Amen, the one who confirms that God is the God of truth and faithfulness.

After the resurrection and ascension, we discover the Lord Jesus bearing this same name " The Amen" — 'the God of Truth'. When He presents Himself to the Laodicean Church, He is the Amen. We read, *"And unto the angel of the church of the Laodiceans write; These things saith the Amen, the faithful and true*

witness, the beginning of the creation of God; "(Revelation 3:14).

Jesus declares Himself to be the Amen, the faithful "God of Truth." His words are steeped with the same divine authority and are as persuasiveness as those of Yahweh because they are one and the same. Christ Jesus is the only one who has entirely understood the mind of God and perfectly executed the will of God. He has authentically demonstrated the character of God and has faithfully and truthfully fulfilled the promises of God because He is God clothed with humanity.

That is why we read in 2 Corinthians 1:20 *"For all the promises of God in Him are yes and in Him Amen unto the glory of God by us."*

Many names are given to Jesus. He is known as, the Light of the World, the Bread of life, the I Am, the Christ, the Good Shepherd, the chief Shepherd, the express image, the Resurrection and the Life, and so on and so forth. Each name is helpful as it tells us something additional about His glorious character, nature and identity. But Jesus is greater than the sum of His names. He is beyond comprehension, He is the very depth of the unfathomable oceans of God's inexhaustible treasures. May we be given grace to explore for riches out of the treasures of the reserves of His names.

Chapter 5

Some Common Objections and Theories Answered.

"But wasn't Jesus merely a good man?"

That's what many folks say-- "Jesus was just a good man; He was a fine upright moral, good man... ... but not God!"

Let's examine that theory against what Jesus actually taught. In John 15:14, He declares; *"You are my friends if you do whatsoever things I command you."* For a mere man to talk in this manner, is to overstep the boundaries of human friendship. If you doubt me, just go to your friends and tell them that from now on you expect them to do everything you command them. Notice, you are not going to ask them to do things, you are, from now on, going to <u>command</u> them....and they are to obey every order that issues from your mouth ...and, if they obey, it will show you that they are you friends. Hey, if you pull a stunt like that, guess how many Christmas parties you're going to be asked to this year! But this is exactly what Jesus did! He says, "You are my friends if you do whatsoever I command you." Therefore, if He were merely a man, He would not have been a particularly good one. In fact, if He's not God, we would have to conclude that he was an arrogant twerp!

What, however, gave Him the right to speak like this? It was one thing, and one thing only; He was God manifest in the flesh. He has a perfect right to command His people to obey because He is God. How say you? Was He a good man or was He God? But remember, if He is not God, then He most certainly was not good!   If He's not God, He's a fraud!

"But wasn't he just an angel?"

Some cults take great delight in telling us that Jesus was an exalted angel. Hebrews 1:6 routes that theory, scattering it headlong. Speaking of Jesus, it says;

"Let all the angels of God worship him."

How can Jesus possibly be an angel since ALL the angels are to worship Him? It doesn't say that most of the angels should worship him but that all the angels of God should worship him. Not a single angel is given a pass on this one. Jesus, therefore, cannot be an angel. If He is an angel, then according to God's command,

He would have to worship Himself!

Furthermore, we know that no angel is to be worshipped since God alone is to receive worship. So let's ask, are the angels commanded in Hebrews 1:6 to worship God or to worship Christ? The text is plain, it is Christ Jesus they are to worship. Are there now two objects of worship for the angels? No, by no means no! They are there to worship God alone (see Psalm 97:7), and this they do when they worship the Lord Jesus Christ!

Furthermore, notice what it says in Colossians 1:16: There we read,

" - all things were created by Him and for Him."

How then does anyone say He is an angel? In the first place, an angel doesn't have the ability to create. He may be able to take something and make something else out of it, but that's not creation. Creation is taking nothing and making something out of nothing ... only God can do that!

In the second place, let's assume an angel actually had the power to create and he created things exclusively for himself, we would again have to conclude him to be an arrogant twerp! What business does an angel have to create anything for himself? It is one thing for God to create things for Himself, but for an angel to do so would be an act of sedition and arrogance.

The point we dare not miss here is that, in the Old Testament, it was Yahweh who created all things for Himself. Proverbs tell us,

"The LORD hath made all things for himself: yea, even the wicked for the day of evil (Proverbs 16:4).

When we, therefore, take Colossians 1:16 together with Proverbs 16:4 we see, once more, that Jesus and Yahweh are one and the same!

Finally, it should also be remembered that the whole point of the book of Colossians is to show the superiority of Christ Jesus over all things. He is not only called the creator (1:16), but He is also the one who is holding the entire universe together, preventing it from disintegration into chaos and confusion.

We read,

"And he is before all things, and by him all things consist (Colossians 1:17).

He is, therefore, again seen as, not a part of creation, but rather, someone superior to and sovereign over all creation and thus superior to all of the angels.

"Some take him a creature to be,

A man or an angel at most:

 Sure these have not feelings like me,

Nor know themselves wretched and lost.

So guilty, so helpless am I,

I dare not confide in his blood'

Nor on his protection rely,

Unless I were sure he was God."

John Newton.

'But wasn't he the beginning of the creation of God? If this is so then he can't be God!"

Yes indeed, He was and is the beginning of the creation of God (see Revelation 3:14). However, before we jump from the indestructible ship of the deity of Christ into the leaking dingy of doubt, we would do well to look more closely at this statement and indeed, the word 'beginning'.

The word "beginning' is the Greek word 'arche' which means 'the Supreme Authority', 'first cause' and 'power'. Arche, designates the source, origin or root of things that exist.

What this verse is, therefore, saying is that Jesus is the supreme authority over and origin of the creation of God (see Michael J. Svigel,

"Christ as 'Arche' in Revelation 3:14," in _Bibliotheca Sacra_, vol. 161 no. 642 (Dallas, TX: Dallas Theological Seminary, April-June 2004).

This verse, Revelation 3:14, this straw fortress of the Arian (JW) cause, does not teach that Jesus was the first-ever created being. In fact, it teaches just the opposite as it affirms that He is the ruler, source, origin and cause of the creation of God. Thus once more, Jesus is seen to be God.

"But doesn't the Bible say He's the Firstborn of all Creation?"

Yes it does! In Colossians 1:15, and following verses we read,

"Who is the image of the invisible God, the firstborn of every creature:
For by him were all things created, that are in heaven, and that are in earth, visible and invisible, whether they be thrones, or dominions, or principalities, or powers: all things were created by him, and for him:
And he is before all things, and by him all things consist. And he is the head of the body, the church: who is the beginning, the firstborn from the dead; that in all things he might have the pre-eminence."

To understand Colossians 1:15-18, it is vital to understand that the term 'firstborn' can mean the chronological order of birth, but it can be equally used figuratively to represent and denote pre-eminence.

In Hebrew culture, when the first child opened the womb, that child was literally the 'firstborn' but when someone was reckoned as being in the place of pre-eminence they were also known as the 'firstborn'--- regardless of whether or not they were the youngest of a large family. This is the figurative use of the term.

Take Manasseh, for example, Joseph's boy, born in Egyptian exile along with Ephraim. Manasseh was called the firstborn because he was literally born first (Genesis 41:51).

However, the second son, Ephraim, is also called the firstborn (Jeremiah 31:9.)

Obviously 'firstborn' here does not mean that he was the one who opened the womb. Rather this means that figuratively he represented the 12 tribes of Israel. 'Firstborn' was, therefore, in this case, a term of pre-eminence. And then of course we have King David. He was the youngest of eight boys, but in Psalm 89:27 the Lord calls him his 'firstborn', higher than the Kings of the earth'. This is clearly a figurative use of the word since David can in no way be understood to be, in any literal time sense, the firstborn of his family.

Since David was neither the firstborn human, nor the firstborn Israelite nor the firstborn in his family we must recognize the title as being figurative, signifying pre-eminence.

Which brings us back to Colossians 1:15 -- *the firstborn of every creature*! We must now ask is the title 'firstborn' being used figuratively or literally. If it is a literal use of the word, then Jesus must have had an actual mother in eternity past. No one in their right mind, however, believes that! This then is obviously a figurative use of the term, designating the pre-eminence that Jesus has over all creation. This truth is further clarified by verse 16. In this verse, Jesus is declared to have the pre-eminence since all things were created by Him and for Him.

"But doesn't the Bible say that it was a man who died and who ascended into Heaven? "

Here is what the verse says,

"But this man, after He had offered one sacrifice for sins forever, sat down on the right hand of God" (Heb 10:12)."

Failing to grasp the dual nature of Christ, His opponents cling in desperation to verses like this. In doing so, they think that they can do great mischief to the truth of Christ's Deity. But like a mouse who tries to whip an elephant with its tail, they fail miserably. "Look," they protest, "it says plainly that Jesus was a man."But of course He was a man, and a good job too! It was a man who died, rose, ascended into Heaven and sat down on His Father's throne.

It was, after all, human beings who needed redemption. An angel could, therefore, not represent and redeem us; we needed one of our own, a human being, to stand in our place. And the good news is, that this man who accomplished redemption was also God. In Christ, and in Christ alone, we have restoration to the Father. Can a mere man bring this about? Can a hard working carpenter from Nazareth be the bridge between God and Man? No, indeed a thousand times no, unless that is, He is God Himself.

Spurgeon tells us that in this verse we see again the complex Person of Christ; " Christ, as God, always was on His Father's Throne. He always was God. And even when He was on earth He was still in Heaven. The Son of God did not cease to be omnipotent and omnipresent when He came wrapped in the garments of clay. He was still on His Father's Throne. He never left it, never came down from Heaven in that sense. He was still there, "God over all, blessed forever." As He has said, "The Son of Man who came down from Heaven, who, also," at that very moment was "in Heaven."   Spurgeon: Christ Exalted: Sermon #91.

But didn't He say something about the Father being His God. How could He be God if He had a God?

That's a great question! Here's exactly what Jesus said;

"Go to my brethren and say unto them, I ascend unto my Father, and your Father; and to my God, and your God" (John 20:17).

The key to understanding this statement lies in the words, *"Go to my brethren."* Now that He had paid for the sins of His people and had risen from the dead, He could refer to all for whom He had died as His brothers and sisters (brethren). Everything that stood between rebel man and the Almighty had been cleared away. Every roadblock had been dismantled and now, speaking as the representative man who had risen from the dead, He could claim His friends as His brothers. Because of the cross, the redeemed are now in covenant with God through Christ. The atonement is complete, and, in Christ, we have a new legal standing with God and have received the spirit of adoption (Romans 8:15).

What a wonderful unfolding of grace there is in the gospel. His followers were at first SERVANTS; then DISCIPLES;

then a little before the cross they were FRIENDS; now, after the resurrection, they are BRETHREN.

When Jesus, therefore, says that The Father is our Father it reveals a glorious gospel mercy to us. Redemption has been accomplished, death dismissed, and now Jesus, in His resurrection, reveals that God is actually Father to those who believe. *"Go tell My brethren that My Father is their Father, and My God their God."*

These are the words of the representative man, the Elect man, and the man who is God. These are the words of our substitute who died and accomplished redemption. As the representative man, Jesus looked to the Father and called him God; likewise, because of the gospel and its tremendous benefits, we now look to God and call Him our Father.

Jesus prophesied that this would happen. He taught that unless a grain of wheat fell into the ground and died it would abide alone, but if it died, it would bring forth much fruit (see John 12:14). Jesus submitted Himself to death, and now, after the resurrection, there is a superb harvest...He no longer abides alone, but has a wonderful harvest, a family of whom He is not ashamed. As Hebrews 2 says; *"For which cause he*

is not ashamed to call them brethren; saying, I will declare thy name unto my brethren;

in the midst of the Church will I sing praise unto thee"
(Hebrews 2: 11, 12).

The 19th century writer W.T.P. Wolston says on this passage;

"----- The feeblest, simplest believer in Jesus has now the same place before God as that glorified Man at God's right hand. For mark, we must have either Christ's place, or no place.----------Humanity is now glorified at God's right hand, and the place Christ has now taken there in resurrection, is the place He has secured for you and me. That place of holy joy and blessedness in the Father's love and presence He shares with all "His own.""

W.T.P. Wolston: The Lord Jesus' 40 Days.

Again, the key to understanding the scriptures that seem to suggest that Jesus is less than God is found in the gospel. The gospel, as you remember, is about the God/Man, Jesus Christ, who He is and what He has accomplished in history on our behalf.

He is God become man. He is God and man in one person. We should always look at the context when reading the words of Jesus to determine whether or not Christ is speaking as God or man. Finally, one astute note on this verse from Jamison, Fausset and Brown;

" I ascend unto my Father and your Father, and to my God and your God—words of incomparable glory! Jesus had habitually called God His Father and on one occasion, in His darkest moment, His God.

-------Yet, note well, He says not, Our Father and our God. All the deepest of the Church fathers were wont to call attention to this, as expressly designed to distinguish between what God is to Him and to us— His Father essentially, ours not so: our God essentially, His not so: His God only in connection with us: our God only in connection with Him. (Robert Jamieson, A. R. Fausset and David Brown Commentary Critical and Explanatory on the Whole Bible, 1871).

But the Bible says He sat down at the "Right Hand" of God...that must mean He is not God!

Here's what the Bible says, *'Who being the brightness of his glory, and the express image of his person, and upholding all things by the word of his power, when he had by himself purged our sins, sat down on the right hand of the Majesty on high" (Hebrews 1:3).*

"But this man, after he had offered one sacrifice for sins for ever, sat down on the right hand of God;" (Hebrews 10:12).

There's a story about a pilot of a small plane who lost his way in a thick fog, and in a state of panic sent out a distress call.

"May Day, May Day... can anyone out there hear me?" The duty officer in a nearby control tower responded, and, after identifying himself, asks, "What is your present height and position?" "I'm 6 ft tall and I'm sitting in the front seat of the plane!"

Misapplying a literal question can be confusing, but, when reading the Bible, mistaking the figurative for the literal brings "confusion twice confounded." This is what happens when we fail to see that the term, 'The Right Hand' is figurative or more correctly, anthropomorphic language. Before looking at the meaning of the term,

"The Right Hand", let's first establish that anthropomorphic language is used in the Bible. When anthropomorphic language is used in reference to God, it represents Him as having human characteristics. We read, for example, of God having "nostrils" (Exodus 15:8), a "face" (Psalms 27:8), a "hand" (Deuteronomy 9:26), and a "mighty arm" (Psalms 89:13). This does not mean, however, that God literally has a face any more than He has wings (Ruth 2:12). We know that God, in essence, is Spirit (John 4:24), but to make Himself more clearly understood He describes Himself in human or anthropomorphic terms. Here, briefly, are 6 anthropomorphic terms to consider.

1. **God's face.**

This speaks to us about God's presence. When we talk about meeting people "Face to Face" it means being in the same place as they are and in their presence. When we seek God's face it means we are seeking to meet him so that we may be in His presence.

2. **God's mighty arm.**

This is His saving power exercised on behalf of people. In Psalm 89:13 we read,

"Thou hast a mighty arm: strong is thy hand, and high is thy right hand."

And in Luke 1:51 we read, *"He hath shown strength with his arm; he hath scattered the proud in the imagination of their hearts."* As you can see, this is not a literal arm. The right arm is usually the strongest.

When, therefore, God intervenes and rescues, it is said to be with His "right arm" or "right hand."

3. **God's hand**.

This expression refers both to God's "call" and to His blessing on a person's life, especially when He gives instruction for ministry.

Ezekiel 1:3; The word of the LORD came expressly unto Ezekiel the priest, the son of Buzi, in the land of the Chaldeans by the river Chebar; and the hand of the LORD was there upon him.

Ezekiel 3:14; So the spirit lifted me up, and took me away, and I went in bitterness, in the heat of my spirit; but the hand of the LORD was strong upon me.
2 Kings 3:15 "But now bring me a minstrel. And it came to pass, when the minstrel played, that the hand of the LORD came upon him."

When we say that the Lord's hand is on someone, we mean that God is directing and blessing that person. We do not mean that a literal hand is resting on the person's head. It is anthropomorphic language.

4. **God's finger.**

This speaks of His commanding authority. In Luke 11:20 Jesus says,

"But if I with the finger of God cast out devils, no doubt the kingdom of God is come upon you."

The demons were not cast out by a literal finger, but by the authority of God in the power of the Holy Spirit.

5. **God's nostrils.** This speaks to us of His indignation!

2 Samuel 22:8-10; "Then the earth shook and trembled; the foundations of heaven moved and shook, because he was wroth. There went up a smoke out of <u>his nostrils</u>, and fire out of his mouth devoured: coals were kindled by it. He bowed the heavens also, and came down; and darkness was under his feet.
Psalm 18:15; Then the channels of waters were seen, and the foundations of the world were discovered at thy rebuke, O LORD, at the blast of the breath of thy <u>nostrils</u>.
The nostrils flare when a person is indignant.

Does God get indignant? Yes! He snorts with anger! Is this literal? No! This is anthropomorphic language. God is Spirit and has no literal nostrils.

The only physical body God has is that of the Lord Jesus Christ.

6) **God's Shoulders**

Deuteronomy 33:11, "The beloved of the Lord shall dwell in safety by Him; and the Lord shall cover him all

the day long, and he shall dwell between His shoulders."
The term "shoulder" signifies strength. Isaiah
prophesies of the birth of the Messiah, saying, *"The
government shall be upon His shoulder"* (Isaiah 9: 6). In
other words, Christ's government will be one of
power and strength.

In Luke 15, in the parable of the lost sheep, the Good
Shepherd finds the stray and lays it on his shoulders.
The shoulders are, therefore, also a place of safety and
rest for the rescued sheep. The sheep are only as safe
as the Shepherd is strong. If the shepherd is weak, the
sheep could yet fall foul of a vicious attack by a wild
beast. We have reason, therefore, for extraordinary
comfort and assurance in the knowledge that our
Shepherd is almighty and that no foe can overpower
Him as He carries us!

When we say that the Lord carries us on His
shoulders, we of course don't mean that He is literally
carrying on literal shoulders. What we mean is that
because we are feeble we look to him to carry us by
His strength and might. An anthropomorphism,
therefore, is a figurative expression that enables us to
relate to God and to understand Him. With this now in
mind, let's turn our attention to the term, 'the Right
Hand of God'. What does it mean?

The first thing we must be clear about is that the Father has no bodily shape! If you think He does, then perhaps you have been reading too many books by the Mormons. We have but one triune God, the Father, the Word and the Holy Spirit.

However, there is only one physical being seated upon the throne, the Lord Jesus Christ, and in Him we will see and encounter the fullness of the Godhead bodily. In Christ alone, we will encounter the Father, Son and Holy Ghost. As the famous puritan, John Owen, said,

"He (Christ Jesus) is the complete image and representation of the Divine Being and excellencies."

John Owen: A Declaration of The Glorious Mystery of the Person of Christ. The Works of John Owen: Volume 1: Page 69.

What then does the term, *"The right hand_"* mean? There are several meanings associated with it. First, it is a hand of <u>Blessing</u>. Consider Genesis 48:17-18; *"And when Joseph saw that his father laid his right hand upon the head of Ephraim, it displeased him: and he held up his father's hand, to remove it from Ephraim's head unto Manasseh's head.*

And Joseph said unto his father, Not so, my father: for this is the firstborn; put thy right hand upon his head."

When we say Christ sits at God's right hand we are saying, not that God has a literal hand, but that Christ is seated in the place of blessing. Furthermore, it is a place of cosmic *Authority and Rulership*. Speaking of Jesus it says,

'Who is gone into heaven, and is on the right hand of God; angels and authorities and powers being made subject unto him (1 Peter 3:22).

The right hand is further seen as the place of <u>Strength</u>. Consider Psalms 98:1,

O sing unto the LORD a new song; for he hath done marvellous things: his right hand, and his holy arm, hath gotten him the victory.

Is the right hand in this verse literal? Did a whopping great hand reach out of heaven and knock the enemy off their horses? Of course not! But when victory is obtained by the right hand, it means that God's authority, power and strength achieved this success.

The right hand is also a place of *honour*: We read;

"Bathsheba therefore went unto King Solomon, to speak unto him for Adonijah. And the king rose up to meet her, and bowed himself unto her, and sat down on his throne, and caused a seat to be set for the king's mother; and she sat on his right hand. 1 Kings 2:19.

Here, the right hand was literal, not anthropomorphic, and it gives us an example of the honour associated with this term.

The right hand is a place of *Power*; we read,

And Jesus said, I am: and ye shall see the Son of man sitting on the right hand of power, and coming in the clouds of heaven. Mark 14: 62

Spurgeon says, "The right hand is the place of power. Christ at the right hand of God has all power in heaven and in earth. Who shall fight against the people who have such power vested in their Captain? O my soul, what can destroy thee if Omnipotence be thy Helper? If the protection of the Almighty covers you, what sword can kill you? Rest secure.

 If Jesus is your all-prevailing King, and has trodden your enemies beneath His feet; if sin, death, and hell are all vanquished by Him, and you are represented in Him, by no possibility can you be destroyed." Spurgeon: Morning and Evening: April 21:Evening.

Furthermore, the right hand is the place of Intercession. He sits at God's right hand, where he intercedes as the High Priest for believers. Consider this; *Romans 8:34; Who is he that condemns? It is Christ that died, yea rather, that is risen again, who is even at the right hand of God, who also makes intercession for us.*

Hebrews 8:1. Now of the things which we have spoken this is the sum: We have such an high priest, who is set on the right hand of the throne of the Majesty in the heavens;

Christ our priest intercedes for us from a position of blessing, favour, honour, power and authority, and as our King applies all the gospel benefits He has obtained for us in His doing and dying.

So, let us summarize. Many people use this one scripture about Jesus being seated on the right hand of God as an excuse for discounting that Christ is God. Now, I don't want to come across as being frivolous or facetious, but think about it. How could someone sit on someone else's right hand for 2000 years? Surely that hand would go to sleep?

For Christ, however, to sit on the right hand of God is a declaration that He is God. He is the one with cosmic authority and power who as the God/Man is seated in the place of favour, acceptance and blessing on behalf of His people.

"But does it really matter if I believe that Christ is God? After all, I love Him and have a relationship with him. Is it, therefore, really important that I believe that he is God?"

Many times I've heard professing Christians talk like that. I have even heard pastors question the value of teaching the doctrine of the deity of Christ. One 'Christian' pastor even told me that writing about Christ's deity was a waste of time as it is not an important subject. Well I'll grant you that if knowing the true and living God is unimportant, then the question of the Deity of Christ is mute. And, if we are not too picky about which god, angel or man saves us, then I suppose that the subject of the deity of Christ is not worth worrying about.

In addition, if it matters not to whom we pledge our loyalty and entrust the keeping of our souls, then this matter of Christ's deity of Christ is a mere tangent of distraction.

Furthermore, if we are not too concerned about which God we worship, then we should pass on to weightier matters. And besides, if we are not too concerned with obeying the first commandment, which the Puritan, John Owen, summarizes as, *"Taking God to be our God"* then I suppose this business of whether or not Christ is God is a theological, trivial pursuit.

However, for the rest of us who care about the truth of the gospel, this doctrine is of paramount value. We are called to believe in the Lord Jesus Christ. But who is He? Is He an angel or a prophet sent from heaven? Just who is this Christ on whom we are to believe? Does true faith latch on to something that is false? It cannot! If it latches unto something false, then it is not true faith. And here's the rub, if there is no true faith, there is no salvation. The person, therefore, who says that Jesus is their Saviour, but they don't believe that He is God is devoid of true, saving faith. Spurgeon has some profound insights on this. He says; "True faith, -- is a faith in Jesus Christ, but it is a faith in Jesus Christ as divine. The man who believes in Jesus Christ as simply a prophet, as only a great teacher, has not the faith that will save him.

Charity would make us hope for many who do not believe in His deity, but honesty compels us to condemn them without exception, so far as vital godliness is concerned. It does not matter how intelligent their conversation, nor how charitable their manners, nor how patriotic their spirit, if they reject Jesus Christ as very God of very God, we believe they shall without doubt perish everlastingly. Our Lord uttered no dubious words when He said. "He that believeth not shall be damned," and we must not attempt to be more liberal than the Lord Himself.

Little allowance can be made for one who receives Jesus the prophet, and rejects Him as God.'
(Adapted from CHS, Sermon 551, Faith and Life).

How Could Jesus Be God if God Forsook Him?

This is a question often posed by those who have not yet grasped the great gospel truth of Jesus, the representative of His people. As the representative man, Jesus was forsaken on our behalf. As a man, He was forsaken, not as God. As a man, He had no sin, but as our representative and substitute He took responsibility for our sins and suffered the forsakenness that sin had earned. As a man, He was treated, as it were, like a poisonous snake, fit only to be trampled and thrown away.

Look at the cross and see Him there suspended between heaven and earth. Look closely at Him and see the forsaken and cursed Man. There He is, lifted up from earth, rejected, despised and acquainted with grief. There He is, lifted towards heaven, but God rejects Him and numbers Him among the transgressors. What an awful sight! The Father lays our sins on Him and treats Him the way we deserved to be treated! He was forsaken for us and as us.

When Jesus Christ was crucified,

The darkness hid His face;

Forsaken there by God and man,

He took the sinner's place.

Transgressors cannot dwell with God,

They have no ray of light;

So Christ saw not the Father's face,

Only eternal night.

Having been forsaken on our behalf, Jesus now stands as the guarantor that the Father can never again forsake His redeemed ones. Our sins can no longer cause God to turn His back on us: we have already undergone God forsakenness at the cross in the person of our substitute.

Everything is finished! Jesus as our representative underwent dreadful torments, the worst of which was a sensing of total forsakenness by the Father. Never was there a more intense and dreadful cry heard than the cry, *"My God my God why hast thou forsaken me"* (Matthew 27: 46).

But, we read the words of this cry and are indifferent because there is hardness in our hearts. We are so dull in the uptake that we fail to grasp the awfulness of this shocking moment. So many of us have not yet grasped the sheer horror of sin. We live with it every day and treat it as irrelevant. But, not so with Jesus: He was a perfect stranger to sin's presence. He neither knew nor committed any sin.

In His ministry, the Father's presence had been His home and dwelling place. He had lived in constant, unbroken enjoyment of the Father's company. He could not think a thought that was out of harmony with the Father's thoughts for their thoughts were one and the same. And since there is only one will in God, His will was always the will of the Father. But here at the cross, as the concentrated fury of heaven's wrath descended upon Him, Jesus cried, "My God, my God, why hast thou forsaken me?" Why indeed? It was because the Lord had laid on Him the iniquity of us all!

Taking responsibility for our sin had broken His fellowship with the Father. God forsakenness is the penalty that naturally and inevitably results from sin --- and Jesus bore it on our behalf.

"His the rejection, the acceptance mine!

 His the vinegar, mine the wine!"

What a horror there was in the cross for Christ! The intimate union with the Father was no longer sensed by Him. For Christ, there was only a staring into the vast chasm of awful separation. No longer was heard the applause and approval of heaven. As Spurgeon said,

"His Father, at that time, gave Him no open acknowledgment. On certain other occasions a voice had been heard, saying, "This is My Beloved Son, in whom I am well pleased."

'But now, when such a testimony seemed most of all required, the oracle was not there! He was hung up as an accursed Thing upon the Cross, for He was "made a curse for us, as it is written, Cursed is everyone that hangs on a tree. And the Lord His God did not own Him before men'"   CHS: My God My God Why Hast Thou Forsaken Me: Sermon # 2133.

The next time someone says to you that the proof that Jesus wasn't God is found in the fact that he cried "My God My God why hast thou forsaken me", do them a favour and teach them the gospel. Jesus, as our representative, walked the valley of the shadow of death alone so that we could say with complete assurance, *"Yea though I walk through the valley of the shadow of death, I will fear no evil: for Thou art with me."*

"But Nobody Believed He Was God Until the Fourth Century!"

If you have a friend who has been duped by Dan Brown and his Da Vinci Code or by some similar piece of fiction, you will have probably heard something along those lines. According to this fashionable fantasy, the Church voted that Jesus would become their God at the Council of Nicaea in AD 325. But what do the facts say? Was the deity of Christ a fourth century invention or a belief held by the church from the beginning? In this and the next section we will show that Christ's early disciples would have laughed at Dan Brown. They knew who Jesus was and, as evidenced by the records of early Christian writings, they continually taught the marvellous truth of His deity. Take, for example, Ignatius (AD 35-117), a disciple of John's who lived 200 years before the Council of Nicaea. When he wrote to the church at Ephesus, he was clear on Christ's identity. He wrote, "Ignatius, who is also called Theophorus, to the Church which is at Ephesus, in Asia, deservedly most happy, being blessed in the greatness and fullness of God the Father, and predestinated before the beginning of time, that it should be always for an enduring and unchangeable glory, being united and elected through the true passion by the will of the Father, and Jesus Christ, our God:

Abundant happiness through Jesus Christ, and His undefiled grace."

Ignatius: Introduction to the Epistle to the Ephesians: (circa) AD107.

In his opening remarks in his Epistle to the Romans, Ignatius also declares Jesus to be the true God when he says of the Roman Church of his day,

"---who are filled inseparably with the grace of God, and are purified from every strange taint, [I wish] abundance of happiness unblameably, in Jesus Christ our God."

Ignatius: Introduction to the Epistle to the Romans: (Circa) AD107.

The early church fathers fervently defended their belief in Christ's deity. Irenaeus, AD 125-202, theologian and Bishop of Lyon, wrote strongly against Gnostic heretics. In chapter 10 of his book *Refutation of Heresies,* he defended the deity of Christ saying, . . . in order that to Christ Jesus, our Lord, and God, and Saviour, and King, according to the will of the invisible Father, "every knee should bow, of things in heaven, and things in earth, and things under the earth, and that every tongue should confess" to Him and that He should execute just judgment towards all.

So much for these 'enlightened' critics who say that the doctrine of the Deity of Christ was a fourth century invention. However, the hatred against Christ Jesus knows no bounds in the hearts of God hating men. Satan will continue to attempt to spew the vomit of hell upon the lovely person of Christ Jesus our Saviour and all the more so as he senses His impending doom.

But the Bible says that no one has seen God!

Here's what the verse says, *"No man hath seen God at any time; the only begotten Son, which is in the bosom of the Father, he hath declared him" (John 1:18).*

Let's look at this verse. This verse terminates the introduction to John's Gospel and summarizes the first eighteen verses of John 1. Christ has "declared"— told out, revealed, unveiled and displayed the Father--- He has exegeted Him. No man has seen God! This means that God in His explosive, glorious essence is so immense that he cannot, without divine intervention, be mediated to men.

However, in this age of grace, God has become visible in, by and through Christ Jesus. In the Old Testament, God was concealed in his secret glory, but now He has been made known and declared in the One who is the express image of His person (Hebrews 1:3).

John 1:18 gives us a remarkable contrast. In the past, God, in the fullness of His glory, was unmanifested. He occasionally appeared in veiled form as the Angel of the Lord, but these were short appearances which did not reveal the fullness of His character. In a very real sense, no man had seen Him; -- but now, God is fully revealed—the Son has "fully declared" Him.

Arthur Pink points out that, "Perhaps this contrast may be made clearer if we refer to two passages in the Old Testament and compare them with two passages in the New. In 1 Kings 8:12 we read, "*Then spake Solomon, The Lord said that he would dwell in the thick darkness*."

Again, "*Clouds and darkness* are round about him" (Psalm 97:2). "These verses do not tell us what God is in Himself, but declare that under the Law He was not revealed. After all, what could be known of a person who dwelt in "thick darkness?"

But now we read in 1 Peter 2:9, "*But you are a chosen generation, a royal priesthood, a holy nation, a peculiar people; that you should show forth the praises*

of him who hath called you out of darkness into his marvellous light." --- A.W. Pink: Christ Eternal and Incarnate.

We are not only called out of the darkness of sin, but also out of the darkness of a veiled knowledge of God.

Again, we read in 1 John 1:5, 7,

"God is light, and in him is no darkness at all ... but if we walk in the light, as he is in the light, we have fellowship one with another."

And this is because the Father has been fully declared by our wonderful Saviour Jesus Christ. In 2 Corinthians we learn that,

"--- God, who commanded the light to shine out of darkness, hath shined in our hearts, to give the light of the knowledge of the glory of God in the face of Jesus Christ" (2 Corinthians 4:6).

Under the dispensation of Law, they lived with a veiled knowledge of God. But the Old Covenant has now passed away, and we live with a full revelation of God in the person of the Lord Jesus Christ. May grace be given us to magnify love and serve the Lord Jesus who has brought us out of darkness into marvellous light. Without Jesus, we would not have been saved; without Jesus, we would not have been ransomed; without Jesus, we would not have been rescued; without Jesus, we would not have been bought out of the slave market. Without Jesus, we will not be brought to heaven; without Jesus, we cannot know God or see Him. Because the God whom no man hath seen at any time, has been fully "declared" in, by and through the Son, the Lord Jesus Christ, we can now see the invisible and know the unknowable. To Him be Glory forever! Without Jesus, God is unapproachable as to His essential being. However, because of our mediator, Jesus the Christ, we can both see and know Him. In the Old Testament, nevertheless, God did appeared and was seen in a limited way. In these appearances, His glory was, of a necessity veiled, for, had it not been, everything would have been consumed. Most commonly,

He appeared as the Angel of the Lord. This was Christ, the Revealer of God, showing Himself in angelic form, preparing the way for His own incarnation.

Let's look briefly at a few of these appearances;

The Angel of the Lord.

That Christ took this form does not mean that He is excluded from being God, on the contrary. The word "Angel" in both Hebrew (malak) and Greek (aggelos or angelos) means a messenger (For a more in depth study on the Angel of the Lord, see www.preceptaustin.org/angel_of_the_lord.htm) Christ Jesus is the ultimate messenger from God; indeed He is God's final word to us (Heb 1:1-3)! He is God's message to us about Himself from Himself!

Notice how the scriptures plainly that this Angel is God Himself. In Genesis 18, He appeared to Abraham in the plains of Mamre, along with two angelic companions. Notice how the chapter begins with the statement, *"The LORD (*Yahweh*) appeared unto him ...."*

Furthermore, as you recall, when Sarah overheard the announcement of the forthcoming birth of Isaac, she, filled with unbelief, laughed inwardly. *"And the LORD (*Yahweh*) said unto Abraham, Wherefore did Sarah laugh...?"*

Then, at the close of the interview, we read, *"and the LORD went his way as soon as he had left off communing with Abraham"* (Genesis. 18:33).

From that time forward, the "Angel of the Lord", the pre-incarnate Christ, constantly appears in the Old Testament preparing the way for His personal appearance as the Word made flesh at Bethlehem.

Consider Jacob, he had the misfortune, or perhaps the blessing, to have wrestled with this Angel at Peniel (Genesis 32). On that occasion, God appeared as a man, fought with Jacob and afterwards Jacob said, *"I have seen God face to face, and my life is preserved"* (verse 30).

Notice again, how this angel was none other than God Himself in a pre-incarnation appearance. We know this for He says so Himself when He declared, *"I am the God of Bethel"* (Genesis 31: 11-13). It was this Angel of the Lord who went before Israel in the wilderness to keep and guide the people of God

and bring them into their inheritance. We read, *"Behold, I send an Angel before thee to keep thee in the way and to bring thee into the place which I have prepared. Beware of him and obey his voice, provoke him not for he will not pardon your transgressions, for my name is in him"* (Exodus 23: 20-21).

That Yahweh's name is in Him, points to the New Testament reality that in Him, in Christ, dwells the fullness of the Godhead bodily (Colossians 2:9).

In Exodus 33:2 God again promises to send "an angel" before His people to drive out the Canaanite,

and also in Deuteronomy 7: 21-24. On this occasion, we learn that it is, *"the Lord thy God, mighty and terrible"* who should be the One who was the promised Angel.

What's more, the One who appeared to Joshua with a drawn sword (Joshua 5: 13-15) was this same Angel whom Moses foretold would drive out the heathen.

Claiming divine privileges, the Angel says, *"As captain of the host of the Lord am I now come.... Loose thy shoe from off thy foot, for the place whereon you stand is holy."* The language that the Captain of the Lord's army uses to Joshua was the same language by Yahweh when confronting Moses at the Burning Bush.

That is why Stephen declares, *"Then appeared to him (Moses) in the wilderness of Mount Sinai an Angel of the Lord in a flame of fire in a bush. When Moses saw it he wondered at the sight: and as he drew near to behold it the voice of the Lord came unto him, saying,*

"I am the God of thy fathers, the God of Abraham, and the God of Isaac, and the God of Jacob. Put off the shoes from thy feet, for the place where you stand is holy ground". (Acts 7: 30-33).

It was Christ, as the Angel of Yahweh, the Eternal Logos, who appeared to Sampson's parents (Judges 13), and *"did wondrously"* by ascending in the flame of Manoah's offering. We read,

"Then Manoah knew that he was an Angel of the Lord ... and Manoah said to his wife, We shall surely die because we have seen God."

As the passage continues, Manoah desires to know the Angel's name. The Angel's reply is of high importance. He says,

"Why askest thou thus after my name, seeing it is secret?" (Judges 13:18).

Don't miss this! The word "secret" is the same word in the Hebrew, translated in Isaiah 9: 6, as "WONDERFUL". Prophesying of Christ, that verse says,"His name shall be called WONDERFUL". In other words, He has the same name as the same God who appeared to Manoah. The true identity of Manoah's Angel was, therefore, Yahweh Himself, the Redeemer of His people. Notice also; the gospel overtones in this episode as the Angel ascends to heaven in the flame of the altar. This angel, by identifying Himself with the offering and ascending in the flames, is a picture of Christ offering Himself for the sins of His people. It is no wonder that He was called 'Wonderful' for this act of Christ in becoming our sacrifice is indeed wonderful beyond words.

Gideon likewise recognized this Angel as the Redeemer of Israel, Jehovah Himself (Judges 6).

"The Angel appeared unto him and said, The Lord is with thee, thou mighty man of valor."

And Gideon said, *'O my Lord, if the LORD (Jehovah/Yahweh) be with us why has this befallen us? ... And the LORD (Jehovah/Yahweh)) looked upon him and said, Go in this thy might and thou shalt save Israel: have not I sent thee."*

So when someone says it is impossible for God to be seen they are only partly right. He can not be seen in the immensity of His entire glory,---no person could survive such a sight! However, the Lord Jesus as our mediator will continually, throughout eternity, reveal the glories of the One True and living God. In the Lord Jesus, there is and will be an unveiling of God in the Person of the Only Begotten who, being made flesh, has declared and made visible the Name and glory of God in Himself. Christ has told out, revealed, unveiled and displayed the Father (John 1:18).

Luther said of John 1:18,

"Therefore all stands entirely on the Son: no man even knows anything of God, but such as is revealed to him by the Son, who fully knows the Father's heart, that the whole world might be brought under the Lord Christ and be subject unto Him; for without Him no-one can be saved." If you are without Christ, you are excluded from the knowledge of God --- for Christ is the declaration of God.

This is an extremely unpopular thing to say in this post-modern era, but I solemnly tell you, if you don't know Christ you don't know God and indeed you are, at this moment, excluded from Him!

In Jesus, Yahweh has become visible. According to John 4:24, God, being a spirit, is invisible. But, in Christ God has made Himself visible. However, the reason for this is not to observe His physical characteristics, but that we would learn about Him, His nature, His Character, His perfections, His faithfulness, His beauty and His Judgment, His holiness and His grace. In Jesus, we see and meet God.

Because of Jesus, we don't need to be in the dark about God. He has gone beyond theory and speculation. He has actually come and pitched His tent in our back yard and invited us to observe and to learn through Christ who and what God is like. When Jesus healed,

 It was God who demonstrated through Christ that He is the healer. When Jesus showed mercy, we were given a revelation of the mercy that resides in the Father's heart. When Jesus taught, He treated us to a splendid feast of the Father's words. Through Christ, we know that the Father is full of grace and truth because Jesus is full of grace and truth. Jesus is the full declaration of the Father.

Jesus is the 'only begotten'. *Only begotten* is rendered in the Greek as "monogenes" and it means "unique"---- or especially beloved. There is no one like Jesus – there is no one like Him in the eyes of the Father. No one can bring us to the Father but Jesus, and He alone brings the Father to us. He is unique. Notice how the Scriptures say He is, *"in the bosom of the Father."*

According to Arthur Pink in his commentary on John's Gospel, the "bosom of the Father speaks of proximity to, and personal intimacy with the Father." It is not, therefore, to be understood, as a literal place or location, but as a state of existence.

According to some scholars, the Syriac version here renders it, *"the only begotten, God which is in the bosom of the Father"* clearly showing, that he is the only begotten, as he is God.

Only the Lord Jesus has clearly and fully declared God's nature, perfections, purposes, promises, counsels, covenant, word, and works; his thoughts and schemes of grace; his love and favour. Again, we must stress that this means that if anyone wants to know God they must come to this knowledge through Jesus Christ. As already mentioned, this is an unpopular thing to say.

If you say it to the people you work with you may be shunned. So are you prepared, as a Christian, to stand up for Jesus? Jesus is our Champion and He is looking for 'Champions' for his cause, champions who will boldly declare his identity and finished work of grace.

And that's the Gospel Truth!

Part 2 of, "Jesus is God. Always was and always will be" contains the following chapter headings,

6) So What Did His Disciples Say?

7) So What Did Jesus Say?

8) Indirect yet Powerful Proofs!

9) Our Man Isaiah.

10) Conclusion.

Biography

Miles McKee is from Maghera, Co. Derry, Northern Ireland. He was raised in a Godly home and became a Christian at the age of 21. He went to the USA and attended Bible College in San Marcos, Texas. He then went on to pastor and church plant in various parts of the World. Miles has had a radio ministry that was heard Worldwide daily and has writes a weekly article which has thousands of subscribers. He is a frequent guest speaker at conferences and churches. He is presently involved in church planting in the Republic of Ireland. Miles now lives in Co. Wexford, Ireland and is married to Gillian.

Miles can be contacted at miles@milesmckee.com

Please tell others of this book (it is also available as an eBook).

If you have been helped by this material, please give this publication a review on Amazon

For more of Miles McKee's writings visit
www.milesmckee.com/books

Other titles by Miles McKee include,

And that's the Gospel truth

Jesus is God ... Always was and always will be:
Part 2

Jesus is God ... Always was and always will be:
Part 3

The Gospel Truth about Jesus

The Gospel Truth about the Blood

Many of the chapters of, "And that's the Gospel
Truth" first appeared in the Wednesday Word.
To subscribe to the Wednesday Word, for free,
email miles@milesmckee.com with the word
'Subscribe' in the subject line.